Advance Praise for

The Voice of the Dolphins

~

Every movement has its genesis, a point where an action seeds an awareness that blossoms into inspiration that evolves into a crusade. In the Seventies, filmmaker Hardy Jones began to focus his eye on the dolphins, in a journalistic odyssey that first exposed the atrocities at Iki and Taiji in Japan, giving birth to this global campaign whose voice has become viral, global and compelling. Hardy's legacy will be a future for these magnificent and intelligent living treasures of the sea.

–CAPTAIN PAUL WATSON,
FOUNDER SEA SHEPHERD CONSERVANCY SOCIETY,
WHALE WARS

~

Hardy Jones has written a book that takes us through the phenomenal, almost unimaginable, world of dolphins in the wild and his thirty-year efforts to protect dolphins from the brutal hand of dolphin hunters and ocean contamination.

–TED DANSON,
ACTOR, MEMBER BOARD OF DIRECTORS OCEANA,
CO-FOUNDER BLUEVOICE.ORG

~

Hardy Jones has been there – in the open sea with friendly dolphins from the Bahamas to South Pacific atolls and at Iki and Taiji, Japan where he has worked to save these marvelous creatures from slaughter. His book is a riveting and highly personal story covering thirty years of extraordinary work. A call to action to save not just dolphins but the oceans and ourselves.

–RIC O'BARRY,
STAR OF *THE COVE* AND INTERNATIONALLY RENOWNED DOLPHIN EXPERT

~

Hardy Jones has an incredible compassion for wild animals. He has put this compassion to work in Japan for over 30 years to save dolphins from slaughter and has saved the lives of literally thousands of these beautiful creatures. Both his films and his writings are compelling and reflect his profound passion for the natural world. This book is a riveting and inspiring true-life story and I urge you to read it.

–CHRIS PALMER,
WILDLIFE FILM PRODUCER, AUTHOR OF *SHOOTING IN THE WILD*.
DISTINGUISHED PROFESSOR IN RESIDENCE, AMERICAN UNIVERSITY

~

Ultimately, this is a story of hope and inspiration from a man whose life has been entwined with the lives of wild dolphins for more than three decades. Hardy Jones has always done what others said couldn't be done: entering the dolphins' world, meeting them on their terms, and reporting back to us through film and in writing. In this vivid, intelligent and timely memoir, Hardy shares his wonder, investigates his concerns, and reminds us that our fates are collectively entwined—whether we are beings of the land or the sea.

–JULIA WHITTY,
AUTHOR *THE FRAGILE EDGE, DEEP BLUE HOME*,
JOHN BURROUGHS MEDAL,
PEN-USA LITERARY AWARD AND OTHER AWARD-WINNING BOOKS,
ENVIRONMENTAL CORRESPONDENT AT MOTHER JONES

~

Hardy Jones is a rare combination of brilliant documentarian, journalist and dolphin advocate who captures the beauty and intelligence of these magnificent beings while educating us about the stunning array of human-made hazards and abuses they must navigate in order to live. And he shows us, in personal and chilling detail, how the fates of dolphins and humans are ultimately bound together.

–LORI MARINO, PHD,
NEUROSCIENTIST AND MARINE MAMMAL EXPERT,
SENIOR LECTURER, DEPARTMENT OF PSYCHOLOGY AND FACULTY AFFILIATE,
CENTER FOR ETHICS, EMORY UNIVERSITY, ATLANTA, GA.

~

Hardy Jones has written an engaging, heartfelt memoir of his life with dolphins that will resonate with any ocean advocate.

–LOUIE PSIHOYOS,
OSCAR-WINNING DIRECTOR OF THE COVE

To my wife Deborah, the wind in my sails, the dolphin on my bow, the love that elevates my life.

To my parents, Hardy and Bobbi, who turned me loose to explore the oceans and who raised me in a world surrounded by love, support and dozens of collie dogs.

The Voice of the

Dolphins

HARDY JONES

Table of Contents

Acknowledgements

I would like to thank the following people without whose support my work and this book would not have been possible: Sakae Hemmi whose unending humor, tireless energy, fierce intelligence, and passionate dedication to protecting dolphins are an inspiration; Ted Danson, a great ocean advocate, who has unflinchingly supported BlueVoice, even before it was BlueVoice; Fred Kaufman, Janet Hess, Bill Murphy at NATURE who gave me the chance to do *The Dolphin Defender* for PBS; Geoff Daniels at National Geographic who green-lighted *When Dolphins Cry*, a difficult and complex film; Julia Whitty, partner, friend, and eloquent voice for the oceans; Dr. Brian Durie at the International Myeloma Foundation, whose energy and keen intelligence has been an inspiration; Jen Nolan and Ingrid Rockefeller, two of the best shipboard companions ever on this incredible journey; Deb Adams for her brilliant and constant support; John Renesch for very early support of my film work with the dolphins; Dr. John Siebel for early support of my work with dolphins and for getting my diagnosis of multiple myeloma right and putting me on the path to stable remission; Deborah Cutting for her keen editorial ideas, her constant upbeat support, and indispensable work for BlueVoice; Chris Palmer, who, when head of Audubon Television, green-lighted three of my films and has remained a friend and advisor for twenty-five years; Andy Sharpless, CEO of Oceana, an extraordinarily competent champion of the oceans; Bill Rossiter of Cetacean Society International, a true friend of whales and dolphins; Howard and Michele Hall, decades-long friends and voices for the oceans; Stan Minasian, a genuine hero in the fight to save dolphins; The Whale and Dolphin Conservation Society; and our dear friend Anonymous from The Boston Foundation.

And finally to the friendly, curious dolphins in the Bahamas who have taught me that my childhood notions of a miraculous universe were far too tame.

Preface

More than thirty years ago, I was swept away into the universe of dolphins. In my work as a filmmaker and journalist, I came to know many of these magnificent animals as individuals, and when I'm with them, I have no doubt that I'm relating to creatures as intelligent, sentient, social, and imbued with emotion as I am. My life became even more closely entwined with dolphins when I learned that we share a genetic trait that imperils both my life and the survival of dolphins worldwide. Ultimately, I came to realize that we share a common fate.

I am not a biologist, and you can find books with much more biological information about dolphins than in this one. This is a personal story. My life with dolphins began when I became fascinated with them at a distance, and then brought a journalist's curiosity to documenting their lives firsthand. From the moment I entered their realm I was enthralled.

This book is also about a battle to save dolphins, whales, oceans, and ourselves from a chemical time bomb that is not just ticking—it is already exploding, albeit in slow motion to our human senses. But I write the book with the belief that we are at a point where we can still turn the tide. More people in more places are aware of the problem. Solutions are at hand, if only we chose to implement them.

This memoir covers three phases of my more than thirty years spent among dolphins and other sea creatures: my initial, exhilarating encounter with friendly dolphins; my subsequent discovery that these creatures are mortally threatened by both slaughter and the chemical contamination of our oceans; and, finally, my diagnosis with a form of blood cancer that has clear links to the same chemical toxins that are causing disastrous consequences among dolphins.

As a boy, during the early days of television, I watched news and documentaries, and I felt the power of transmitting the spoken word coupled with pictures to millions of people. I wanted to be one of those who delivered the news, and after serving in the Peace Corps from 1966 through 1968, I went to work for CBS News during its glory days, as a researcher, a reporter, and eventually a news director and anchorman.

But after three years of living that dream, I left the news business to become a natural history film producer. I wanted to tell stories of particular interest to me in my own way. In a paroxysm of naiveté, I decided to make a film on dolphins— not in aquarium tanks but in the open sea. The depth of my ignorance was profound, but if I'd been better informed, I would never have set out to make that first film. Precisely because I knew nothing of the failures of those who had gone before me, including Jacques Cousteau, I threw myself into this quixotic adventure of finding and filming a school of dolphins in the wild with never a thought of failure.

While researching this project in 1976, I learned of two dreadful threats to dolphins—tuna seiners that killed hundreds of thousands of dolphins each year in their fishing nets and the drive hunts in Japan that killed dolphins for food or just to wipe out a species that "eats too many fish." What began as an intense fascination with dolphins evolved into a desperate crusade to save them. My first effort was to make a documentary film about dolphins in the wild.

In 1978, the save-the-whales movement was just gaining traction. Through sheer persistence and dozens of phone calls, I learned of a school of unusually friendly spotted dolphins in a remote area of the Bahamas. I raised some money, found a partner, brought together a film crew, and set sail. We found the so-called *Maravilla* dolphins, named for a Spanish galleon that had sunk in 1656 on the western edge of the Little Bahama Bank, and I began a relationship with this school and many of its members that lasts to this day.

Starting with the film that came from this first life-changing encounter, I have made dozens of films about marine mammals for PBS, National Geographic, and Discovery Channel, as well as for France's Canal Plus and other foreign distributors. Filming became my entrée into the world of dolphins but was not my ultimate purpose there. My true aim was to get inside the minds of these animals in whom I sensed a unique intelligence. In coming years, I would apply what we had learned with the spotted dolphins to killer whales in the arctic fjords of Norway and to sperm whales off the Galapagos Islands and the Caribbean island of Dominica. I became a pioneer in a parallel universe inhabited by highly intelligent, friendly, curious aliens. I came to love them and felt an intense need to protect them.

The International Wildlife Film Festival in Missoula, Montana, is one of the most important annual events for wildlife film producers. It's where you go to make deals with television commissioners from PBS, National Geographic, and the BBC. I'd attended the festival often in the past, shown some of my films, given keynote speeches, and met old friends in from the wild.

But at the end of April 2003, the idea of traveling to Montana for the festival seemed more than I could manage. For the past year, I'd been having mysterious symptoms, including heart arrhythmia, debilitating fatigue, muscle pain and weakness. Recent blood tests showed I was severely anemic and pointed to worse. I anxiously awaited the results of a bone marrow biopsy that would likely lead to a diagnosis of a serious disease. I was in pain, weak, and afraid. I told my wife Deborah I didn't think I could make it to the festival.

She said, "Of course you should go. Don't sit around worrying. Being with your friends will be great for you."

I called my friend and physician, Dr. John Siebel, sniveling that I was afraid of being exposed to germs on the plane or in public meetings when I might have a weakened immune system. He ridiculed the idea. "That's bullshit. Get on up there, and I'll take care of you when you get back."

Reluctantly, I went. I pushed myself to go to festival events. One was a panel of film commissioners speaking about what they were looking for in a film. When it was over, I approached one of the panelists, Janet Hess, supervising writer of the splendid PBS series NATURE, with an idea for a film on the latest amazing discoveries in the world of dolphins. She seemed mildly interested and asked me to send a proposal to her at WNET-TV, the PBS affiliate in New York that produces the series.

A week after returning home to San Francisco, I was diagnosed with multiple myeloma, a form of blood cancer that has no cure, and had to decide whether to undergo a radical stem cell transplant. The transplant would have incapacitated me for months and mean I would have had to give up all work and income. The alternative was a combination of two drugs that had just become available. To me, there was really no choice. I didn't want to undergo a procedure that involved massive doses of chemotherapy and so chose the so-called novel therapies. I struggled with their side effects, but my first lab tests after beginning the regimen came back with stunning results. The two drugs had reduced my burden of monoclonal (cancer) cells by 98 percent.

By the time I started writing the proposal for NATURE my condition was improving rapidly. My blood counts were acceptable, and my heart was beating normally. I wrote a proposal and sent it to Janet with video clips from all the dolphin films I'd done over the previous twenty-five years. My proposal was about the latest discoveries from the world of dolphins—recent experiments that proved they have the capacity for self-recognition, new feeding strategies discovered in Australia, and so on. The treatment was two pages long. I put together a reel of footage I'd shot over the years but debated whether to send shots of myself interacting with dolphins, especially clips of things like an underwater piano and the Macintosh computer we'd put into a waterproof case to record and play back sounds. How would the executives at a highly prestigious series like NATURE react to film of me playing T-shirt tag with a group of spotted dolphins? But I decided to throw it all in. "Fortune favors the bold," I thought and laughed to myself as I sent it off.

Janet came back to me quickly. "We don't want to do a film along the lines of your treatment."

"Damn!" I thought.

"But we want you to do a film on your life with dolphins. We want all the personal and emotional elements told in the first person, including those underwater computers. Can you do something like that?"

Well, I guess I could!

In follow-up conversations with Janet and her colleagues, we mapped out the general shape of the film that would be an episodic journey through my career of making films about dolphins. It would combine archival footage shot over a period of several decades with newly shot footage that would fill in gaps in the story and bring it up to date. That part gave me pause: I had no idea how I would hold up physically under the stresses of shooting underwater and all the travel involved. My first task was to see what I already had to work with and how it might all fit together. I hadn't looked at a lot of that old film for years, and as I started to screen bits and pieces, memories flooded back with a combination of exhilaration, nostalgia, and not a few thoughts of how young I looked. The reaction was, no doubt, intensified by my new-found sense of mortality.

The film would be titled *The Dolphin Defender*. How did I get to be him?

~ 1 ~

When Dolphins Were a Dream

My first encounter with a dolphin can be seen on a fuzzy home-movie taken by my mother in 1957 at the Miami Seaquarium. I was sixteen years old and vacationing with my family in Florida. We walked around the park looking at flamingos and monkeys, but it was the dolphins I wanted to see.

We entered the dolphin stadium and climbed the cement steps through dark passages smelling of cotton candy and hot dogs. Once we were out in the sunlight, there was a blue, water-filled tank the size of a large swimming pool. But it contained no dolphins. Suddenly there was a musical fanfare; a couple of people in white, knee-high boots ran out onto a platform; and four dolphins burst from a cramped holding area into the main tank in a series of spectacular leaps.

The show they performed was thrilling. Sleek, athletic dolphins dove through hoops, kissed members of the audience, and, as though they were rocket propelled, accomplished astonishing vertical leaps to touch a ball suspended above the tank. Judging by their smiles, the dolphins were having a marvelous time. When it was over, I was reluctant to leave and lagged behind with my mother and father, brother and sister, while the rest of the audience left the small amphitheater.

When the stands were empty, I went to the side of the tank, stood on my toes, and leaned over the rail. Immediately a dolphin appeared, rising out of the water in front of me, making a high-pitched sound like a creaky door. The dolphin's smile was infinitely inviting, and it kept jerking its head as if to say, "Come on; let's play." I remember feeling honored that this extraordinary creature was paying attention to me.

But what could I do to respond to the invitation? I looked right and left. There was a garbage bin nearby, next to the "Do Not Throw Anything to the Dolphins" sign, and I pawed around in it until I found an empty black plastic 35-mm film canister. I looked both ways to be sure no one was watching then threw it toward the dolphin, who launched into the air and snatched the object in its jaws. It ducked underwater, then stood on its tail and threw it back to me. I tossed the canister higher, and the dolphin leaped, picked it out of the air, and in the same motion tossed it to me before reentering the water with barely a ripple. All the while, it was creaking and whistling. I tried to encourage this behavior by imitating the vocalizations.

I was thrilled with the game we'd so quickly evolved together and was looking for something better than a film container to throw when one of the trainers appeared and ejected me and my family from the stadium. I looked back over my shoulder and imagined the dolphin was disappointed. Despite the apparent smile on its face, my dolphin friend's eyes seemed lonely. The trainers then coaxed all the dolphins back into the cramped holding tanks, and I realized that was where they spent their time when not performing. It would be a long time before dolphins reentered my life.

I was not engaged with my studies during my school years at Choate, a prestigious New England prep school. What riveted my attention were books by Jacques Cousteau, Eugenie Clark, Hans Haas, and other ocean explorers. I was enraptured by descriptions of the underwater world and was determined somehow to experience it for myself. Mental images of Cousteau in deep aquamarine waters off the Cape Verde Islands contrasted starkly with the dark Connecticut winters and what I saw as a banal way of life my parents seemed to have in mind for me.

One of my favorite authors then was Bob Marx, a treasure diver and marine archeologist. My favorite among his long list of published books was *Diving for Pleasure and Treasure*. Nineteen years later, Bob Marx would lead me to a treasure that would totally alter my life.

After a stint in the Peace Corps in Peru, I realized my childhood dream of working at CBS News. I came on board as a researcher but even at that lowly level had contact with Walter Cronkite, Dan Rather, and a wonderful reporter named Richard C. Hottelet, who ran the CBS bureau at the United Nations.

I worked in the election division and the space unit where I pulled all-nighters listening to the squawk from the space vehicles headed to and from the moon. For the launch of Apollo 11—the first mission designed to put a man on the surface of the moon—CBS sent our space unit to the Johnson Space Center in Houston, Texas.

I was in the broadcast studio as Walter Cronkite described the momentous event. As the Apollo 11 crew approached the landing spot at Tranquility Base, Mr. Cronkite yelled out that he needed a "think piece" to put the landing in context. I took a shot at it, tapping out something about the similarities between the moon mission and the forays in tiny vessels by the Iberian explorers who had rounded the Cape and discovered North and South America. Cronkite glanced at it and put it aside, but a few minutes after the immortal words, "Houston, Tranquility Base. The *Eagle* has landed," he took my thoughts and integrated them seamlessly into his on-air presentation. I was elated.

The correspondents at CBS were giants in my mind. They had been imprisoned by the Nazis and had parachuted into Europe on D Day or in Operation Market Garden. By and large, they were kind and helpful to me as I learned the business of reporting honest and objective news. My time at CBS News allowed me to mix with presidents and princes and taught me the valuable lesson of persistence in running down a story.

But even as I thrilled to the assignments I got at CBS—the space unit, the election unit, a post at the United Nations, I knew something was missing; something inside me demanded attention. I left CBS News in 1972 and went to California at the time of the explosion of interest in self-awareness and personal development. I spent time in ashrams, in Zen centers. I did *est* and other seminars dealing with human potential. Confident that something would emerge if I gave it time, I was content with being directionless for a while.

Among the leading gurus of the day was Dr. John Lilly, a neuroanatomist who believed he could establish communication with dolphins using a computer. Lilly spoke of self-reinforcing belief systems and used dolphins as a counterpoint to humans. "It is difficult to learn about ourselves because we are ourselves. We have to have a point of reference outside ourselves to really understand who we are. If you ask a fish about water, the fish would say, 'what water?' because all it knows is water."

During long afternoons in a small cabin perched above the cliffs of Big Sur, Lilly explained how interaction with another species—a species with the right measure of similarities and differences relative to humans—might help us in the process of self-exploration. The species he nominated for that role was the bottlenose dolphin, a creature both similar enough to us to allow comparison to human behavior and different enough from us to offer points of contrast:

"Dolphins have similarities and differences with human beings that make the comparison worthwhile. Both species are highly intelligent, social, and have complex abilities to communicate. But humans have hands and can manipulate the world—dolphins don't. Humans live in gravity and give over much of their computational capacity [brain power] to avoiding falling. Dolphins live in a world of zero gravity. Humans are primarily visual creatures with an enlarged visual cortex. Dolphins are creatures who perceive their world by a kind of sonar and have highly developed acoustical cortexes."

Lilly spoke of the brain structure of humans, dolphins, killer whales, and sperm whales. The bottlenose dolphin, he said, has a brain a third larger than the human brain and every bit as complex. The point to which he returned again and again was that if an animal has a large brain, it must be doing something very important with it. Large brains are metabolically "expensive" and must do something that enhances survival, or they would not have passed the trials of evolution. Sadly, he said, that while studies had been done of dolphins in captivity, we knew virtually nothing about how they use their huge and complex brains in the wild.

An excitement began to build in me that was almost uncontainable as Lilly pointed out that we humans had once believed the earth was flat and that the sun revolved around it. Astronomy had taught us that was not true, but he went on: "Most of us still believe we are the only creatures on earth with a mind and a soul." He made a compelling case, based on the anatomy of the dolphin brain, that we are, in fact, not alone in these capacities, and he suggested we do not need to travel to the far ends of the universe to find other forms of intelligence. Dolphins, he said, are, in more ways than one, extraterrestrials, creatures with highly evolved nonhuman intelligence, living just off our shores.

At the feet of the master, I had a cognitive breakthrough. I would go to sea, find dolphins, study and film them, and bring this miraculous information back to land-based humanity. My world took shape in an instant. I could return to the ocean with a purpose.

In 1976, not long after my first encounter with Lilly, Governor Jerry Brown of California sponsored "A Celebration of Whales and Dolphins," an all-day series of films and speakers in Sacramento. I attended and marveled in the deepest levels of my soul at the magnificent images of whales and dolphins at sea and then was sickened by films that showed whales being harpooned and dolphins dying literally by the millions in the nets of tuna fishermen.

My sense of being directionless morphed into a ferocious hatred for the men who killed whales and dolphins. Plans raced through my head every time I closed my eyes: throwing Molotov cocktails onto the tuna fishing boats based in San Diego, swimming the fierce currents of the Golden Gate to bring attention to the issue, somehow sabotaging the whaling ships. That mental venting was nonsense. I had to find something that would actually transform the situation—and for a man of my skill set and experience, that something was to make a film showing the world so clearly the wonder of dolphins and whales that the killing of them would be seen as an atrocity and would be quickly brought to an end. My naiveté was both my greatest ally and my greatest liability. I would go into the open sea, meet dolphins in the wild, and film their societies, personal interrelationships, and awesome grace and beauty.

I wanted to get to sea and film dolphins in their own element. I recalled the impact of the great CBS documentaries such as *Hunger in America* and hoped to achieve something on that order of magnitude for dolphins. And the community that had grown up around the human potential movement in San Francisco was the perfect environment in which to raise money to save a highly conscious species such as dolphins. Consciousness was the name of the game in those days.

Back at my home in Sausalito, I began investigating what it would take to film dolphins in the open sea in hope of recording behaviors that would illustrate Lilly's thesis and vastly expand the perceptions people held about dolphins. I read all of Lilly's books and several of Cousteau's. Cousteau had described capturing a dolphin in the Mediterranean and watching it ram into the walls of the containment pool repeatedly until it died. It was heartbreaking and a good argument against captivity.

For all he did to raise awareness of the oceans, there was a ruthless side to Cousteau. On one hand, he would write of dolphin intelligence and yet could still harpoon a pilot whale so he could check its stomach contents. He had also killed dozens of dolphins to use as bait to incite shark feeding frenzies in front of his cameras. Those events took place in his early days and, taken in their best light, illustrate how far we have come in our awareness of dolphins and whales.

I reviewed the history of human relations with dolphins and whales, reading *Mind in the Waters*, a compendium of essays on whales and dolphins through history. I learned that the ancient Greeks had laws making it a capital crime to kill a dolphin. But no one had explored the dolphins in their own domain. This only stoked my desire to meet them in the open sea.

At a seminar I produced featuring Buckminster Fuller, I met filmmaker Michael Wiese and explained my idea of heading into the open sea to film dolphins. I wanted to capture the lives of free-swimming dolphins in a way that would help end the killing of dolphins in the tuna fishery. We became partners on the spot. Michael was a genuine filmmaker. He knew about cameras, about how to put together a crew, and what film stocks would work in which environments. I brought the documentarian's point of view to the film—journalistic accuracy and hard information on dolphins and the oceans. A combination of naiveté, enthusiasm, and determination to end the killing of dolphins got us started and kept us going. If we had thought there might be a chance we would fail, we would never have put to sea.

We set out to find the dolphins with a mind-set that the structure, complexity, and size of their brains proved these are creatures that love, remember the past, are able to project into the future, and have a sense of ethics and morality, just as humans do.

And so on the fourth of June 1978, Michael and I, along with a film crew, set out from Marsh Harbor in the Bahamas on the *William H. Albury.* I stood on the bowsprit feeling just short of ecstatic. My lives as newsman, scuba diver, consciousness student, and dolphin lover had fused into one. And there was a story to be told of magnificence and innocence juxtaposed with brutality and bloody horror.

Now we just had to find a school of approachable dolphins in the vastness of the open sea.

~ 2 ~

First Contact – Conversation with Dolphins

A couple of years earlier, the likelihood of my being able to film dolphins in the wild had been ridiculed. When I discussed the idea with marine mammal experts, they scoffed. No one had ever been able to stay with dolphins underwater in the wild long enough to film or study them. Occasionally, a single dolphin would befriend humans in some remote place like New Zealand, but except for these rare and unpredictable occasions, dolphins didn't seem to like people in the water with them. They'd ride a ship's bow wave but leave whenever a diver went over the side. Even Jacques Cousteau had never been able to film dolphins underwater in their natural setting. "*Absolument impossible*," he told me dismissively. The advice of the experts was unanimous: if I wanted to do a documentary on dolphins, I'd better film it in an oceanarium.

The other option was to do a more journalistic conservation film on the plight of dolphins. The straight reportorial route was the genre I was accustomed to and didn't require doing something everyone agreed was impossible. But I had learned as a reporter that if you pick up a telephone and start asking questions, you'll eventually be led to the answers you need. I called all over the world, asking, "Do you know anywhere a person could film a school of dolphins underwater in the wild?" For a long time the results were discouraging: "It can't be done." "*On ne peut pas.*" "*No se puede hacer.*" But after weeks of fruitless phone calls, I got a tip from Stan Minasian, a young marine mammal conservationist. Stan had made the film *Last Days of the Dolphins*, the horrifying story of six million dolphins dying in the tuna fishing nets that I'd seen at Jerry Brown's "Celebration of Whales and Dolphins" event. He told me of a treasure diver, Bob Marx, who'd taken some astonishing film footage of a uniquely approachable school of dolphins in the Bahamas. Somehow, his name sounded vaguely familiar. I called him at his home in Florida.

At first, he denied even knowing about such dolphins, but when I told him my purpose was to save the lives of dolphins, he conceded that he knew a school of spotted dolphins in a remote area of the Bahamas that were remarkably curious and even friendly. But he remained suspicious. "Why do you want to film my dolphins? I don't want anyone going out there just to cowboy around."

I convinced him that I wanted to make a film that would help end the massacres of dolphins in the tuna fishery, and that was enough to earn me an invitation to join him on his boat off Marathon Key, Florida, where he was searching for treasure.

On the plane to Florida, the name Bob Marx kept running through my mind. And then I recalled *Diving for Pleasure and Treasure* by one Bob Marx. I remembered how stories of his exploits, read under the covers by flashlight after curfew, had transformed my Spartan boarding school bedroom into a staging area for future adventures. This, I thought, must be the author of that book.

In those days, the Florida Keys had not yet been overbuilt. In an air-conditioned Hertz rental car, I drove along Route 1, which connects the keys like a string of pearls, as far as Marathon; then, I turned left down a dirt road and opened the windows. The air was so hot it felt like it would sear the lungs. I drove past boats up on blocks. The smell of paint and varnish and sand blast was in the air. Men without shirts were applying huge rotary sanders to boat bottoms and picking pieces of machinery out of holds, stopping frequently to wipe their foreheads with oily forearms and swill down beer and cola. It was not yet ten o'clock in the morning.

I reached a dock and walked out to the end where Marx had said I'd find his treasure-salvage vessel. It was about one hundred feet long with two huge curved funnels hanging off the stern used to excavate the bottom. I knocked on the railing, and a fierce, bronze face thrust out of the salon door, squinting into the morning light for the source of the intrusion. Treasure divers don't like people poking around their boats.

"What the hell do you want?" were his first words. He was tall and blondish, with a belly that revealed he didn't mind a good meal or a toddy from time to time. He was muscular as well, and his skin was tanned mahogany and wrinkled like tortoise hide from decades of looking for treasure in the tropics. Yet, his face was strangely smooth, and his eyes seemed to peer out from deep inside his skull. I realized he'd had a facelift.

Marx looked every bit a buccaneer—and sounded it. In an effort to take the edge off his rudeness, one of his crew murmured that Bob might be having one of his bad days. Marx heard him and, by way of his reply, imparted his philosophy of life: "There are good days, and there are bad days. The good days are when you find treasure." Even for a world-class treasure diver like Marx, that must have made for a lot of bad days.

Looking for a way to get on his better side, I asked if he'd ever written a book.

"A book? I've written twenty-six books."

That was impressive.

"*Diving for Pleasure and Treasure,* right? I used to read it under the covers when I was in prep school." I said.

He nodded and even smiled but then scoffed. "Christ, I've got a preppy on my boat!"

But when he started to talk about dolphins Marx's rough facade cracked then fell away entirely. His story was fascinating and he loved telling it. He'd spent a decade exploring a remote part of the Bahamas searching for the wreck of the seventeenth-century Spanish galleon *Nuestra Senora de las Maravillas*. During the course of the search, a school of uniquely friendly Atlantic spotted dolphins had been attracted to the holes the treasure divers blasted in the sand. When the sand blasters excavated areas of the bottom, they opened a smorgasbord of bottom-dwelling fish for the dolphins. Over the years, the dolphins' curiosity and friendliness had increased to the point that Marx saw them almost every day.

The story of the ill-fated ship, as Marx told it, was chilling: The *Maravilla* had departed Vera Cruz, Mexico, on December 24, 1655, en route to Spain with an immense quantity of gold, silver, and precious stones dug up in Mexico and South America. She also carried a life-size, solid gold statue of the Madonna. The value of the treasure in today's terms would exceed $200 million dollars.

Part of a large treasure fleet, the *Maravilla* had traveled seven days through the Straits of Florida before turning north along the western edge of the Bahamas, her progress aided by the three-knot flow of the Gulf Stream. On New Year's Eve, the passengers and crew celebrated, excessively. Early the following morning, as they slept off their revelry, a lookout spread the alarm. The *Maravilla* had drifted into shallow waters. She turned desperately for the open sea only to collide with another ship of the fleet. As she drifted back onto the banks, she hit a reef and broke in half. The bow settled immediately on sand and reef twenty feet below while the stern drifted southward.

The Spanish crown was not easily reconciled to the loss of so vast a sum of treasure, especially the statue of the Madonna.

During the following three summers, they sent divers to search the shallow waters of the western Little Bahama Bank. These attempts resulted in the retrieval of only a small portion of the treasure. During the recovery operations a story circulated among the salvers: Of a complement of seven hundred men aboard the *Maravilla*, only fifty-six had survived that fateful New Year's Day. It's possible that while bobbing at sea waiting to be rescued, one or more of them had seen dolphins. In any case, while researching in the *Archives of the Indies* in Seville, Spain, Marx came upon a legend that the *Maravilla* crew members who had perished had been transformed into dolphins. Not averse to mixing fact with whimsy, he implied that the friendly dolphins inhabiting the area today might be their descendants.

By the fourth year of the seventeenth-century salvage effort, the wind and seas had covered the wreckage with sand, and though the salvers searched for her location for another twenty years, *Nuestra Senora de las Maravillas* remained lost until the 1960s, when Marx found information in the *Archives of the Indies* that allowed him to relocate the wreck. He was able to recover only half the treasure, then worth about $20 million, and he desperately wanted to go back and get the rest. But during a quarrel over division of the spoils, he had insulted the prime minister of the Bahamas and was declared *persona non grata*, so he was relegated to working the Florida Keys.

Once he'd told his story, Marx's mood changed again. "So what the hell do you want with me?" he growled. But by now, the toughness seemed forced.

I wrenched myself back from my imaginings and told Bob about the tens, even hundreds of thousands of dolphins drowning in the tuna nets each year—some of them spotted dolphins. He'd known about the problem but was appalled to learn how many were being killed. It made him furious, and it made him my ally. He deliberated three seconds, shrugged slightly, then pulled out a navigational chart and pointed to a spot.

"North of Grand Bahama on the Little Bahama Bank, there's a spot I've been going for more than twenty years. This spot is about forty miles from the nearest land. It's a primitive area. Nobody fishes out there. Tourists don't go there. Diving parties don't go there. And that's because there's not a reef or any place where you can get safe anchorage. No matter which way the wind's blowing, you're exposed to it.

"That's where we found the *Maravilla,* and almost every day while we were searching and digging, we'd be visited by a school of spotted dolphins who were so curious and friendly they'd swim right up to ya. After a while, they'd drift off if you didn't keep them interested. You go there and you'll find them. I've never told anyone this, and if you don't do what you say you're gonna do, you'll wish we'd never met."

I wanted to know the odds the dolphins would be there if we chartered a boat and brought out a film crew.

"One hundred percent. I've seen 'em every time I've been there. When you come up on pure white sand, you'll know you're there."

I copied the latitude and longitude, traced the important part of the map, thanked Marx, and went off to figure my next move. Glancing down at the point indicated on the map, I thought, "X marks the spot," and laughed. Should I throw the dice based on Marx's word? Any better ideas? I was elated that we had a lead to friendly dolphins and that I'd met a boyhood hero who'd been everything I could have hoped for. But I was a long way from actually finding those dolphins. For one thing, we needed about fifty thousand dollars to put together a film crew and to charter a suitable vessel.

San Francisco in the late 1970s was the perfect spot to raise money for such a project. Many investors thought our quest to be spiritual. Others just wanted to be connected to dolphins in some way.

My partner, Michael Wiese, an independent filmmaker with a new-age inclination, and I set up a limited partnership; did a few presentations to people who had disposable income; and raised the money to do the initial filming. Some of our new partners had attended my seminars and been inspired by a new way to look at themselves and the world.

Investors would receive a percentage of profits should we succeed in making the film and selling it, but these people were far more motivated by a genuine desire to do good and were fascinated by the prospect of being a part of opening communication with dolphins in the open sea and by saving countless thousands of dolphins from death.

One of the first investors was John Siebel, then practicing emergency room medicine. John and I had met at Choate and spent hours contemplating marvelous adventures we would have when we got loose in the world. We maintained close contact over the years. While I was finishing Tulane undergrad and working in New Orleans, he was at Tulane Medical School. He came down to visit me in Peru when I was serving in the Peace Corps, and we'd traveled through the Andes into Bolivia. John was my oldest friend and surfing buddy. He's a truly original thinker with a wonderful combination of imagination and skepticism that lets him separate the true miracles of life from meaningless fantasy. He's also an extraordinary free-diver, and I wanted him along to be the one person who could swim with the dolphins without having any other task to distract him. I convinced Michael that it would be good to have a doctor on our expedition, and so John sailed with us.

Once the budget was raised, we set out to assemble a filmmaking team. Michael was the film guy. I was the reporter and dolphin "expert." Our topside shooter was John Knoop, who, hand-rolled cigarette dangling at his lips, looked like a young

Humphrey Bogart. Steve Gagne, a wild-haired former roadie for the Grateful Dead, was our sound recordist. There were two women in the complement: Morgan Smith, a pretty New England girl who had captured Michael's heart, and Mary Earle, whose mother had invested in the film.

Now that it looked like we might be able to find dolphins, the problem became what to do when we found them. Our concern was how we'd keep the dolphins interested in us long enough to get the kind of film footage we needed. But beyond a general need to get beauty shots of the animals and sequences of interaction between them and humans, we had no shooting script. No one had ever done this before, and we just didn't have any idea how it would unfold.

Steve Gagne drew on his rock music and acoustical expertise and sketched a scheme for what he called "an underwater piano." He planned to enclose the mechanism of a sound synthesizer in a waterproof Plexiglas case. The instrument would be powered by the exhaust from his scuba apparatus, and he could make a form of music by fingering a keyboard.

At first, the concept struck me as ludicrous. The contraption looked like something Rube Goldberg would have come up with on two cups of espresso. I was very uncomfortable with the new-age notion of playing music to wild animals and was thoroughly skeptical that it would work. I wanted to make a film that would be taken seriously. But I had a lot to learn.

We would meet our charter vessel at Marsh Harbor in the Abaco Islands in the northeastern reaches of the Bahamas. She was the *William H. Albury*, a seventy-foot, gaff-rigged schooner out of Man-O-War Cay, a genuine tall ship, white hulled with two masts, the last of the Bahama trading schooners converted into a yacht for charter. Our underwater film crew flew into Miami from various points around the globe, and we assembled at Tamiami airport for a charter flight to rendezvous with the boat.

The first to arrive was underwater cameraman Jim Hudnall, who flew in from Maui. Jim had made a name as the first person to film humpback whales underwater. Astonishingly, no one had been in the water with these animals until the mid-1970s. It's hard to imagine what those first moments with the whales must have been like. No one could predict their reactions to a human entering their realm. The film work he did for National Geographic introduced a breath-taking new idea to the world: whales are not sea monsters or leviathans. They're gentle and graceful animals, curious toward humans in the water. Jim's work had come at a time when whales were being hunted to near extinction all over the world, and helped turn public opinion against the ghastly business of whaling.

Our other underwater cameraman was Jack McKenney. He turned heads when he pulled up at the wing of our Aerocommander in a Pontiac convertible driven by an extravagant blonde wearing short shorts and a low-cut bikini top. He was an extraordinary looking guy, about six-feet-six tall, lean, and muscular, with a close-cropped and meticulously etched beard in the style of a Greek statue. He slung his gear onto the tarmac and kissed the woman in the convertible good-bye. As she drove off, he wiped some metaphorical perspiration from his brow and flicked it away with his fingers.

At two in the afternoon of June 4, we touched down at the tiny airstrip at Marsh Harbor. By 4:00 p.m., we'd transferred the gear and cast off aboard *Albury*.

The weather is brutally hot in the Bahamas during the summer, and that day was no exception. The late-afternoon light was highly saturated, casting the surface world in gold. Towering cumulus clouds contrasted sharply against the deep blue sky. The ship was captained by Mike Cochran, a pleasant guy with a full beard, and crewed by two young Bahamians, Ray Manni, a swarthy Sicilian, and deckman Ray Weatherfield, a tow-headed nineteen-year-old, who was part of the small population of white people who inhabit the Abacos, descendants of Tories who'd fled the United States during the War of Independence to remain under the British Crown.

Also aboard was a guy who called himself Ric O'Feldman, a former trainer of Flipper. He would later rename himself Ric O'Barry and transform himself into one of the world's most effective agents helping dolphins.

We planned to motor-sail the first evening and make it as far as we could before dark. Our target for the second night was a group of wash rocks called Double Breasted Cay. We'd be on the location Marx had indicated by the end of the third day. It turns out the choice of *Albury* was born of ignorance. Our destination was just sixty miles from the coast of Florida, and we'd have done far better to cross the Gulf Stream than to sail the entire 180-mile length of the Little Bahama Bank.

You can't sail the shallow and largely uncharted waters of the banks at night, so as our first evening approached, we anchored off Green Turtle Cay and swam in the enchanting light that comes just before the sun touches the horizon in the tropics. The water was warm and very salty. A sense of tremendous satisfaction and contentment filled us all. We had made it. We were on our way to the dolphins.

We broke out some rum and fruit juice, and as we had dinner on deck, we began to talk of what had brought us to this moment. I filled in the details of how we intended to make a documentary that would help save the lives of dolphins in the tuna fishery. But even as I rattled on about "my purpose," I knew I was looking for something far beyond making a documentary film or even saving the lives of dolphins. I struggled to describe it, especially to myself. I couldn't, but knew I'd recognize it when I found it.

Members of our group drifted off, some to load cameras, others to sleep. John Siebel and I poured another cup of rum, sat back, and sighed with satisfaction. We were living the adventures we had dreamed of while at Choate.

We sailed the next day on the outside of the Abacos on the deep ocean in rolling seas, our tender, a sixteen-foot Boston Whaler bobbing and thrashing in the swell off the stern. Michael was seasick and spent most of the day on his back, showing signs of life only by occasional dashes to the rail. To our left were the low, sparse islands which constitute most of the Bahamas: Ambergris Cay and Stranger's Cay, as well as places that exist only at low tide, like Grouper Rocks.

The second night, we tucked in at Double Breasted Cay, a long and narrow island buffering the northern edge of the Little Bahama Bank from the swells of the Atlantic Ocean. The island was a breeding area for some kind of tern, but I couldn't identify the species. When I asked Ray Weatherly what kind of bird it was, he replied matter-of-factly.

"Them are egg birds" which came out "Thim uh igg buds."

"Egg birds?" I asked.

"Yeah, Igg buds."

Thinking he might have misunderstood my question, I asked him, "What bird species are they part of?"

He looked at me as though I were hard of hearing or mentally incompetent and answered as articulately as his thick Abaco accent would allow. "Th're Igg buds. Igg...buds." He walked over to a nest, scaring the parents into flight, and plucked out an egg.

Taking a tack that I thought might illuminate my question, I asked what kind of egg he was holding. His answer cut short any hope of further enlightenment.

"Th're Igg Bud iggs. Ya eat 'em," he replied.

On day three, we sailed across the final segment of the banks in water so shallow we occasionally had to put a snorkeler over the side to check the depth under the keel. Several times there was no more than six inches clearance, and if there'd been any swell at all, we'd have broken the keel of the ship on the hard bottom. The heat sapped us of our energy and intention. Down below, it was a sweatbox with no air moving. Topside, the shade from the sail shifted with each move of the boat. A sense of delirium descended on me. Then the water deepened. A breeze brought welcome relief. I raised my head then stood grasping the stays.

At five in the afternoon of the third day, we reached the northwest edge of the Little Bahama Bank where it intersects the Gulf Stream, the location Bob Marx had indicated on the chart. It was only then that the preoccupation of gathering the film crew, chartering a boat, and sailing across 150 miles of shallows gave way to the realization that I didn't know Marx from Adam. He might be a man with a sense of humor. We might have been sent on a preposterous wild-goose chase. And I remembered his remark about the dolphins up here being descendants of lost mariners. Not exactly hard fact.

The sun was twenty degrees above a horizon, scalloped by clouds edged in pink gold. The depth of the water went from twelve feet to twenty-five, and the bottom turned from irregular small coral heads and patches of sea grass to pure white sand. Amazing sugar white sand! The wind and swells continued to build. I scanned an empty ocean.

As the bow of the *Albury* rose and fell, cleaving a path through the swells, a phalanx of dolphins appeared, porpoising down the golden path made by the low-angled sun reflecting off the sea. They came flying out of the tops of the six-foot swells, droplets of liquid gold streaming behind them. They came at us with unfettered energy and unreserved curiosity and with a grace, speed, and power that filled me with awe.

Marx had not misled us. The dolphins were there—right where he'd said they'd be. And they were spotted dolphins, just as he'd described. For an instant, we all stood transfixed, then cheered at the top of our lungs.

Captain Mike did his best to keep our bow into the wind, but this meant our side was to the swells, so the boat rolled hard. Above us, the masts swung violently tracing thirty-foot arcs in the sky.

The seas were too high to put the underwater piano over the side, but the dolphins were there and we were desperate to get footage, so Jack McKenney and Jim Hudnall threw on scuba gear and grabbed their cameras. I stood on deck holding mask, snorkel and fins, trying to get a sense of what was going on and thinking I ought to be directing something. But all was chaos—dolphins arriving and disappearing, our crew crazed with excitement, the wind building, the boom tearing on its fetters, and the ship rocking wildly in the six-foot swells.

The sun was just a few degrees above the horizon when we entered the water, a time when predators rouse themselves for a night of feeding. But if we even gave this a thought, we were buoyed by a naïve confidence that the dolphins would protect us. I timed my entry to jump into the crest of a swell. In six-foot seas you fall six feet from the deck level to water level and another six feet into the trough. So you can fall twelve feet and then have the boat land on your head.

I swam hard to get clear of the hull. The water was 83 degrees. For the moment, all I could see was clear blue water and pure white sand twenty feet below. Then half a dozen dolphins streaked toward me. Some were densely spotted. Others were a clean gunmetal color. All had bellies flaming pink with excitement. From this first instant, it was clear something extraordinary was happening. The dolphins did not flee. Senior males, heavily spotted, raced in to sonar me, then disappeared only to return with females and juveniles. They'd evidently concluded that we were so slow and clumsy in the water, that we were harmless.

I swam to Jim and Jack, who were spinning in circles, trying to figure out which group of dolphins to film. "Just get something on film. Shoot anything. This may be our only chance," was my desperate instruction to them.

Within five minutes, the entire dive team was in the water. Cameramen rolled out their film loads on the nonstop action, then surfaced and screamed for the Boston Whaler manned by Ray to take them back to *Albury* to reload. For the next hour, as the sun dropped below rose and gold cumulus clouds, we swam in the warm, clear sea with these creatures we had come so far to meet. Beneath us, the white sand gleamed, illuminating both dolphins and humans and providing enough light to permit filming.

Groups of divers and dolphins were alternately surfacing and diving. Everywhere there were fins and flukes; gray dolphin dorsal fins and suntanned human backs; snorkels, flippers, and blows.

Dolphins raced at me from all directions, their eyes wide and bloodshot with excitement. The sea was a cacophony of breaking waves, my own gasping, yells, outboard motors, and the creaky-door buzzing of dolphin sonar. Whenever I surfaced, I tried to get some idea of how the filming was going, but no one was even remotely coherent. Words tumbled out of ecstatic faces.

"Incredible!"

"I've never seen anything like this."

"Dolphins. Dolphins. Dolphins everywhere!"

Those of us without a camera worked to establish contact with individuals or groups of dolphins. We swam and dived with no thought of where the mother ship might be nor with any other thought of safety. In this vast, featureless area of shallow ocean, we oriented to the dolphins. Where they went, we tried to follow. When they left, we tried anything to lure them back: splashing, yelling, swimming fast, and diving. Being with the dolphins overwhelmed all other considerations.

After the first minutes of exhilaration, I began to focus, to look at the dolphins and to see details. The majority were about six feet long, the largest perhaps seven feet in length. The smaller ones were a pure, luminescent steely gray. Larger members of the pod had individual spots, and on the largest of them, the spots merged into patterns that covered their bodies. The radiant, pearly color of the newborns reflected light and allowed us to see them much farther away than the spotted adults. I wondered whether that coloring let their parents spot them quickly in times of danger.

A group of nine very large dolphins, swimming in formation, stacked and shoulder-to-shoulder, approached me. They were packed as tightly as a fistful of cigars. The tips of their beaks were brilliant white, and they seemed to have a serious demeanor about them.

One thing was obvious: these creatures were as conscious of me as I was of them. I looked into their eyes, and they looked back, inquisitive, excited, friendly. These were not the eyes of a shark, interested only in whether there's a potential meal about, nor even the eyes of a friendly dog. In the eyes of the dolphins, I could see keenness, even an analytical process taking place. This perception was not a hard fact like the length of body or color of skin, but it was very, very real.

Their faces held a hint of the dolphin "smile," though not as pronounced as in the bottlenose dolphin. I had to remind myself that the configuration of their faces was evolution's design, giving them maximum hydrodynamic efficiency, not the expression of emotion. But I couldn't escape the message radiating from their deep brown eyes—"We're excited that you're here. We're interested, amused. We are not afraid." My perceptions were supported by their behavior.

We were, I thought, aliens, clumsy, slow, almost helpless in the water compared to the dolphins, dropping through the surface of their fluid, blue universe. At worst, we were like the circus coming to town. At best they saw some signs of intelligence in us.

I made a surface dive and swam down among a mixed group of juvenile and adult dolphins, blending into their formations, banking and turning in mid-water. It seemed I had no need to breathe, that I'd assumed properties of a dolphin just by being among them. When my air did run out, I clawed my way back to the surface and gasped for breath, often to find a trio of dolphins accompanying me. Below, John Siebel swam over the white sand in the midst of no fewer than fifteen spotted dolphins, each twisting and craning its head to examine him.

As the sun touched the horizon, Captain Mike saw his shipmates scattered to all points of the compass and sent the Boston Whaler out to retrieve us. But no one would be retrieved. Anyone who'd lost contact with the dolphins boarded the whaler only long enough for dolphins to appear on the bow, then leaped overboard again. Aboard *Albury*, Mike was screaming against the wind. No one cared.

The whaler careened among snorkelers surfacing and dolphins rolling their backs for a quick breath before rejoining the melee below. It was only chance or some beneficent spirit of the deep that kept someone from being killed. We all survived the madness of first contact only because the dolphins vanished just as the sun dipped below the horizon.

I stared into the clear Bahamian waters. Now there was only sand below and an empty deepening blue. The dancing shapes, the incarnations of animal spirit, our elegant and energetic new friends were gone. I swam back to the boat, floating not in the sea but in a sense of delirious joy. Ordinary life, with its mix of distraction, nonsense, and trepidation, had been annihilated by the experience of being in this untrespassed place among dolphins. This was an experience that made a lifetime worthwhile.

Diver after diver timed the swells to scramble up the swim ladder and onto the heaving deck. Normally, this can be a real challenge in turbulent seas like this, but on that day, we could all fly. Once on deck, wide eyes that had only moments ago been fixed on the dolphins, now stared inward, mind focusing on an experience each was unwilling to leave.

As night fell and the swells continued to build out of the northwest, we began to sort out dive gear and cameras. Brief conversations occurred as one diver asked another "Did you touch them?" "Did you see the babies?" "How close did you get?"

And the answers came back: "They came charging at me."

"I think the one with the spots really liked me."

And more than anything else, "We gotta do this again."

In almost everyone's recollections there was mention of one particular dolphin.

"Did you see the one with the remora attached to its side?"

"Yeah, it swam with me the whole time."

"It swam with me!"

"It swam with me too!"

The night brought lightning in the distance and rumbles of thunder over the water and still stronger wind. Adrenaline spent, exhaustion came upon all of us, and we sat in the main salon as the squall approached.

I remembered what Bob Marx had said about these waters: "You're out there in the open. No shelter from the weather. The wind blows one way, the current pushes another, and the Gulf Stream can push up waves ten feet tall."

It had just started to rain, and there were calls to close the hatch. Captain Mike stood at the top of the nearly vertical ladder leading from the salon to the deck. There was a blinding flash of lightning and an explosion of thunder so near that the two events seemed to happen simultaneously. I blinked and Captain Mike was standing twelve steps below where he'd been. One instant, he was at the top of the stairs; the next, he was standing down in the salon, a negative image in lightning-blinded eyes. Mike was stunned but not damaged.

Some of the group ate a bit and went to sleep. As the sea heaved the ship in an ugly fashion, a few became seasick. The *Albury* spent the night hauling at its anchor line like a huge, relentless dog on a tether. It was an uncomfortable night, hot, sticky, and rough.

By morning, the wind had dropped and we ran on a northerly course in fifty feet of water on a flat sea over a bottom mottled with coral heads hoping to pick up dolphins on the bow. The water was so clear sea fans were distinguishable on the sand below. For hours, there was no contact. By late afternoon, we wondered if our experience of the day before had been a unique event. The sun at 4:00 p.m. was 30 degrees above the horizon. The light was getting richer, more saturated, "tastier" as filmmakers like to say.

An oily gleam of light, a disruption on the surface of the calm sea, a gray torpedo hurtling toward our bow, a cry of "Dolphins!" from one voice, then from half a dozen. It was a sequence that would occur countless times in years to come yet never become routine.

Dolphins intercepted our course, and took up positions on both sides of the bow, keeping pace with barely a flick of their tail flukes, pushed along like surfers by the pressure wave made by *Albury's* forward motion. We cruised for ten minutes and shot two magazines of film, but there were only so many ways to photograph the same action. Then Jack McKenney had an idea: he and I could hang by our arms from the rope off the witch's cradle under the bowsprit and suspend ourselves in the water to share the bow wave with the dolphins. It might scare them off, but it might be seen as initiation of a game.

With barely a thought that if we lost our grip, we'd be run over and pulled through the ship's propellers, we lowered ourselves into the glassy waters. The dolphins barely reacted, moving only slightly to the side or ahead of us. After a moment, they settled back into their former positions, including Jack and me in their formations. I was beyond ecstatic. I had passed through the looking glass and entered a parallel universe.

Two dolphins swam just in front of me, mottled shadows two feet under water. Another surfaced and blew just an arm's length to my right. The warm, salty Bahamian waters lifted us, and the pull of the boat allowed us to skim along the surface. My arms felt strong. The sun made the world warm with golden light. I wanted to freeze or distill this moment to somehow hold on to it.

I stuck my head underwater and rolled to the side. The dolphins became excited and barraged me with sonar. A youngster bolted in from the stern wake and nearly touched me before its mother called it away. More dolphins arrived, and now it was clear we had reached the middle of their territory, so Mike slowed the boat and Ray dropped anchor. The dolphins lingered and began to play among themselves only a few feet from *Albury*. My own private moments with the dolphins came to an end as the rest of our crew jumped into the water. Excited, the dolphins responded, pink bellies flashing against the deep turquoise background.

We swam with the dolphins as the sun melted into the horizon. Jack and Jim filmed, but the rest of us sought out individual dolphins. Both dolphins and humans were more relaxed than during first contact. The mood of the encounter reflected the calm clarity of the sea. Perhaps we had gone through the introductory stage of excitement and wonder and could now begin to get to know one another in a calmer mood. We looked the dolphins in the eye, and they looked back. Although it was only a day after our first meeting, it felt like a reunion in the open sea, more than thirty miles from land.

I tried to sort out a protocol for being in the presence of dolphins to learn what they considered appropriate and what might offend or scare them. I found that when I descended on breath hold twenty feet to the white sand bottom and then swam tangentially toward the dolphins (not directly at them), they would welcome me into their group. Then, when I needed to rise to the surface for breath, the entire subgroup of which I had become an honorary member would follow me up and breathe synchronously. I tried to take a single breath in a fluid motion at the surface and then immediately dive again as the dolphins do, but was soon so winded I had to stay ten to twenty seconds at the surface gasping air and hyperventilating. The dolphins would remain patiently with me, and when I arched my back for another dive, they were clearly pleased and shot to the bottom to resume playing or looking for snacks in the sand. It seemed that the fact that both species were free-diving allowed each to recognize the commonality of our shared need for air.

Finally, I turned my head and noticed the medium-sized dolphin with the remora, or suckerfish, swimming about three yards from me making a series of whistles while expelling air in a thin trickle from her blowhole. I looked straight at her (we learned her sex a year later), and the two of us locked eyes. She slowed to match my swimming speed and neither averted her eyes, nor veered off. As long as I looked her in the eye, she stayed practically glued to my flank. We swam linked in this manner for perhaps sixty seconds. I was transfixed by the dolphin's serene, unchanging face and felt as though I was looking into the eyes of a Buddha. Unable to hold my eyes open any longer because of the sting of salt water, I tried a method of communication I've used with cats. I blinked both eyes, holding them shut for a beat. When I opened them, the dolphin had closed her eyes to very narrow slits and seemed to be smiling.

When I lifted my head out of the water to locate *Albury*, the spell was broken. But I had learned something: making eye contact could produce a remarkable connection between human and dolphin. This is very different from what would happen with other species. Staring at a dog will appear as a threat or challenge. Staring at a bear or mountain gorilla can provoke an attack.

The only disruption that afternoon was a large barracuda that darted among the swimmers, a reminder that we were in an environment not entirely benign. I was sure that it was just curious, but it made Mary and Morgan nervous. From time to time, dolphins would chase it off, but the 'cuda kept returning to gaze at us, occasionally opening its mouth to reveal its toothy armament.

As the sun dipped below the horizon, the dolphins departed again, and we gathered at the bottom of the swim ladder. Each of us had a moment to reflect and drink in the warmth, the color, and the knowledge that we had again made friendly contact with intelligent creatures who were not human. It set the mind ablaze.

On the morning of day three in the dolphin zone—our fifth day at sea—the swell had built to four feet and the sky was overcast, but conditions were workable. Captain Mike wanted to get back to Marsh Harbor as soon as possible so we didn't have to run over the banks and reefs at night. But we had not come this far to leave without trying the underwater piano.

There were no dolphins in sight when we began to make ready for Steve's piano concert. We'd already solved the problem of attracting the dolphins. But playing music would be something that might raise their curiosity a bit, and if anything happened, it would make a great scene in the film.

As Steve prepared his gear, Ray went back to bail out the whaler and found a dead barracuda in the bottom of the boat. No one could explain how a barracuda might have gotten there. We hadn't been fishing. Could it have jumped in by accident? Then I noticed the dead fish had a set of teeth marks on its dorsal side behind the head that matched the shape of a dolphin jaw. The only possible answer seemed to be that one of the dolphins had somehow killed it and placed it in our dingy. Was this the barracuda that had been annoying some of us the previous afternoon? Could the dolphins be concerned about our safety or even our state of mind? Was it a joke or a display of their powers? That mystery would last several years before later events led to a plausible answer.

The camera team put on scuba gear and slipped into the water. John lowered what we called "the piano" over the side to Steve, who was worried the rise and fall of the swells would slam his precious instrument against the hull and damage it before he could put it to use. The instrument was essentially a keyboard attached to a synthesizer with an underwater speaker clipped to the side. This was housed in Plexiglas, just like underwater cameras of the day. Steve held it in his hands. Nothing connected him to it except a line from his scuba tank. The contraption was about the size of an accordion. It weighed nothing when in the water but was slightly awkward and subject to the currents.

He pushed off from the side of the boat, exhaled, and descended, regulating his breathing to provide air to power the instrument. Although there were no dolphins in sight, Jack and Jim assumed positions to film.

Steve was kneeling on the bottom at a depth of about eighteen feet when he began playing. A couple of minutes passed, and nothing happened. I was looking around and wondering whether I should associate myself with this bizarre undertaking. Five minutes passed. Steve was still playing, but I was already shaking my head and mumbling to myself that I'd never really thought this music business would work. I walked to the bow . . .

A squadron of dolphins appeared, moving at phenomenal speed, flying more than swimming. They covered three hundred yards in a matter of seconds, and when they reached *Albury's* bow, they dove, wheeling and turning around the source of the music.

For Steve their arrival came as a complete surprise. The film footage Jack shot shows him snapping his head up and left as the dolphins flew past him like fighter jets on a strafing run. He changed his music instantly from fugue to a kind of polka, and pushed off the sand to swim about six feet above the bottom. The dolphins took up positions just ahead of him and matched their speed to his as though they were enjoying the show. Before long, dolphins and humans had calmed, and if you didn't think too hard, all that was happening was that a man with an underwater piano was playing a concert for a school of dolphins thirty miles from the nearest land.

Aboard *Albury*, all we could see were rippling dark shapes against the white sand bottom. But it was clear that the dolphins were staying very close to Steve. And the cameras were rolling.

A group of four young dolphins swam slowly just in front of the Plexiglas box, leaving only long enough to rise to the surface for a breath of air, then gliding back to be near the music. Six older dolphins swam in the mid-water, curious but unwilling to approach as closely as the juveniles. They kept up a steady but relaxed stream of clicks and whistles, occasionally flicking their tail flukes and whistling with some energy. Steve felt they were attempting to interact with his music through their vocalizations but he couldn't be sure. The sounds dolphins make are at the upper range of human hearing and we register only a tiny fraction of their vocal output. In addition, it's difficult to determine which dolphin is vocalizing at any given moment. Sound travels five times faster in water than it does in air, so the ability we normally have to directionalize is lost.

After half an hour of hard breathing, Steve returned to *Albury* for a fresh tank of air along with the cameramen who needed to reload. Scuba tanks were changed and camera housings dried and opened so magazines could be swapped out.

The dolphins lingered around our boat roughhousing among themselves. Steve came on deck. He didn't want to wrestle with the underwater piano any further. Now he wanted to sing into a microphone connected to underwater speakers hanging from the boat's starboard side. It would be another experiment. He crooned a few phrases. We looked up and the dolphins had vanished. Steve looked very hurt. But at least we were learning what dolphins like and don't like.

With the dolphins gone, Captain Mike began to organize us for the return to Marsh Harbor. As we hauled anchor and took up an easterly course, I stared at the unbroken, featureless surface of the sea. At an earlier time, I might have described the scene as desolate, but now I knew that beyond this looking glass was a world peopled by friendly and curious dolphins.

I remember little of the return trip to Marsh Harbor. Michael and I were convinced that we had a fantastic film in the can. Nothing like this had ever been filmed before. But more than that, my thoughts were of the dolphins themselves. Visions of individual faces and memories of moments of contact played behind my eyes as I stared, without focusing, at the sea, the outside world barely a distraction.

I tried to sort out what the dolphins had communicated and what that implied for future contacts. They'd come from the open reaches of the sea to the bow of our boat. That said they liked to bow ride. But they'd been known to do that since men first put to sea. They had not run off when we entered the water and had swum within inches of us. They even allowed their young to swim within arm's length. That surely said they were not afraid of us. They had come to the music we played. That indicated they were curious and oriented to sound. So they were curious and unafraid—not a bad beginning for a relationship. They'd stayed around for more than an hour on each of our three encounters. That would seem to mean they enjoyed our presence. As I thought about it, it seemed their feelings about us resembled ours for them.

And, finally, there was their response to eye contact. The female with the remora had locked onto me when I'd turned my head to look directly at her. What did that mean? Babies lock eyes with their mothers. Lovers look into each other's eyes. It was a response that seemed to say, "I see you and I see that you see me." It said, "Someone is at home over here," and that was a good beginning to a relationship, one that would last for decades.

I felt that we had opened a dialogue and made some friends. The contact was ending far too quickly. I would have been sad if I hadn't already been planning my return.

~ 3 ~

The Sea Runs Red

Over the next eleven months, Michael and I assembled the footage for editing. As we screened it, we noticed things we had not recognized during the adrenalin-fueled hours with the dolphins. We saw that bubbles streamed from their blowholes as they approached us making short and repetitious vocalizations. We didn't know the term then, but those were signature whistles. Essentially, the dolphin was introducing itself to us. I felt dumb as I realized we had not responded to an introduction. We hadn't known enough to reply to them.

Michael and I differed sharply on the tone and content of the film. He wanted to include suggestions that dolphins might be psychic while I insisted we needed a rigorous documentary that would stand up to scientific and journalistic scrutiny. Eventually we arrived at a film that was lyrical but didn't venture into new age thinking.

The film, titled simply *Dolphin*, was made at a time when people, especially in California, were moved to action by the idea that such a film could save the lives of hundreds of thousands of dolphins. This was not a scientific film. We aimed it straight at hearts and minds.

In June 1979, *Dolphin* opened to a sold-out audience at the Palace of Fine Arts in San Francisco. The film startled scientists. Some were enthusiastic; others, clearly antagonistic.

The footage showed that behavioral studies on dolphins could be done in the wild. Dolphins would no longer have to be captured or killed to be studied. More than that, the footage showed dolphins as they had never been seen before in the wild: curious, friendly, playful, and affectionate among themselves and with us. The footage would revolutionize the way scientists and the public viewed dolphins and would raise ethical questions about how we must treat them.

The film expressed the idea that, since dolphins have large brains, intricate social systems, and friendliness to humans, we ought to treat them as a special case, giving them legal protection against killing, capture, and degradation of their habitat. But once you do that with one species, you open an ethical Pandora's box that has no clear boundaries. One way out of the conundrum is to realize that protecting dolphins requires protection of the ocean habitat itself to the benefit of all marine creatures, not to mention human beings.

At the Society of Marine Mammalogy Conference in Seattle in 1979, I showed some of the footage. A few of the scientists were interested, but the majority mocked our approach. They accused me of lacking objectivity and of anthropomorphizing—in their eyes, the hideous crime of allowing that dolphins might share common traits with humans.

Dr. Roger Payne, one of the most respected marine mammal scientists of our day came to my rescue. Payne had been the first man ever to record the songs of the humpback whale. Seizing the microphone at the front of the auditorium, he addressed the group. "What you have just seen is the future of marine mammal science—going out into the sea to observe and catalogue the behaviors of animals in their own environment. This film is a great service. It expands our horizons. And I can tell you that if you don't get out of the lab and out among the study animals, someone else will."

In the years since our first encounters with the spotted dolphins, the techniques used to make *Dolphin* have been widely adopted. Scientists now enter the water to observe the subjects of their studies. They use videotape and still photography to identify individuals and catalogue social behavior. Indeed, the attitude of many marine mammal scientists has expanded to allow that dolphins and humans may share many traits in common including emotions, culture, and altruism. But at the time, it was nice to have Roger Payne on our side.

Dolphin aired nationally on PBS in December of 1979 and was eventually seen by some 20 million people in the United States and by millions more in international broadcasts. The project was a great success from a personal point of view. But it didn't stop the slaughter of dolphins. It didn't visibly change the world. That would be a longer, slower process with intricate convolutions and an astonishing array of characters, some of whom started as villains and ended as allies.

But for now we did have a film with a powerful message and I began to think of ways to use it both to help dolphins and as a way to return to the Bahamas. Working with the *Maravilla* dolphins was exquisite and, if this were a better world, could easily have occupied my entire professional lifetime. But I felt that studying and filming the spotted dolphins in the idyllic world of the Bahamas could never be more than half the mission.

This was brought home to me with shocking force when, midway through 1978, a friend showed me a news photo of a brutal slaughter of dolphins that had recently taken place on a small island known as Iki, off the southwest coast of Japan. The photo, taken from the air, showed hundreds of dolphins dead on a beach and hundreds more confined in nets awaiting the blade.

Japan was and continues to be viewed by many as an environmental villain. Not only has she been the leading whaling nation, but Japanese fishing practices also decimate populations of fish around the world by using devastating long-line and gill-net fishing techniques. The slaughter of dolphins was perceived as another outrage.

Of course, Japan is not the only nation ravaging the planet but steadfast unwillingness to compromise on issues such as whaling, the importation of turtle shells and elephant tusks and opposing limits on the take of bluefin tuna has branded the *Land of the Rising Sun* as rapacious and uncaring.

Again and again, especially in early morning hours when I couldn't sleep, my thoughts returned to the brutal images of dolphins piled on the beaches of Iki, and I began reading in-depth about the situation there. I placed an aerial photograph of the dead dolphins littering the beach at Iki on my desk. Next to that photograph, stood a framed print of two dolphins, looking at me as we swam side by side in the turquoise waters of the Little Bahama Bank.

The contrasting images reminded me that each of the dolphins entrapped in a net at Iki was the equal of individual dolphins I was coming to know in the Bahamas. For me it was both a blessing and a curse that I could imagine so keenly the horror of similar creatures being driven from the sea and butchered in nets half a world away. The two photographs were a guarantee that I would not forget those murdered dolphins or the ones who would inevitably follow them onto Iki's bloody beaches if I did nothing.

I began to investigate the history of the dolphin killing at Iki. The island's residents, predominantly Buddhist, live simple lives based on the sea. Until the mid-1970s, they were prosperous, owing to their proximity to the Shichiriga Banks, one of the most productive fishing areas around the Japanese archipelago. From these waters, they pulled abundant quantities of yellowtail and squid. Those waters were also on the migration route of vast squadrons of dolphins—bottlenose, huge gray and white Risso's, and jet-black false killer whales.

Throughout the 1970s, though, the fishermen had experienced a decline in their fish catch that threatened to wipe out their traditional way of life that until then had been in harmony with the local environment. They found their catch of squid and yellowtail were declining. They suspected dolphins were taking too many fish. In the mid-1970s, a Japanese scientist, Dr. Toshio Kasuya, visited the island and estimated the number of dolphins passing through the fishing grounds at three hundred thousand. He told the fishermen how many fish each dolphin ate. The number computed was astronomical, and the fishermen quickly translated the total pounds of fish eaten by the dolphins into lost catch, money out of their pockets, and food off their dinner tables.

The fishermen's response to this information was to begin shooting and harpooning dolphins, but though they killed a few, the effort was ineffectual. So they searched for another, more "final solution". In 1977, they adopted the *oi komi* dolphin drive, a technique used by fishermen in other parts of Japan who hunt dolphins for food. When dolphins are sighted, the fishermen form their boats, each of them made of white fiberglass and roughly thirty feet in length, into a huge horseshoe on one side of the dolphin pod. They swing metal pipes into the water and bang on them with hammers and steel rods. The clanging from a hundred boats or more curling around the dolphin pod in a U-shape causes the dolphins, with their exquisitely sensitive hearing, to flee ahead of the painful sound. Maintaining communication through CB radios, the fishermen maneuver the horseshoe so as to drive the dolphins into a bay where they can be confined and killed by stabbing them with long spears.

In 1977, the fishermen of Iki held their first dolphin round-up and killed a few hundred bottlenose dolphins and false killer whales. In 1978, they did it again and killed eight hundred more. Then they made a colossal mistake. The fishermen were so confident of the righteousness of their cause that they invited a television reporter from the mainland to witness the killing. The fishermen had hoped the reporter would tell the world, Japanese fisheries officials in particular, about the problem the huge number of dolphins was causing to innocent fishermen and their families.

The reporter came to Iki with a television cameraman who shot film footage from a helicopter as the fishermen drove spears into hundreds of dolphins and the waters turned blood red in the bay below. A still photograph made from the movie film was flashed around the world and was published in hundreds of newspapers. Environmental groups were alerted to what was happening, and some protests took place, but for most, the story died. Iki is a remote place.

The terrible irony of this story is that the people of Iki had formerly revered the dolphins that migrated through their waters each spring. They actually called Iki "The Island of the Happy Dolphins." Researchers who had visited the island reported the fishermen had built a shrine to the dolphins they killed and there were other indications that what was going on was something larger than a thoughtless massacre. The more I learned, the more I began to think this was a story with universal implications that needed to be told.

As the fall of 1978 progressed, I increasingly felt the pressure of knowing that within a couple of months dolphins would again appear on the Shichiriga Banks off Iki looking for fish.

Buoyed by the success of *Dolphin* and filled with desperation about the fate of the dolphins at Iki, I began working the phones and eventually put together a group of investors to finance a new film, one that would show not just the horror of the dolphin slaughter but also the factors which turned otherwise decent people into killers. Again, I turned to the "consciousness community" around San Francisco for funding. Part of my promise to my investors was that they would be helping save the lives of hundreds, even thousands of dolphins.

I reassembled the production team from *Dolphin*. John Knoop was the natural choice as shooter. He's widely traveled and has a marvelous eye for detail and mood. Steve Gagne agreed to do our sound recording. But Jack McKenney was unavailable for the underwater work. He suggested Howard Hall, a young underwater cameraman whose work had impressed him during production of the feature film *The Deep*. I gave Howard a call, and he signed on. It was the beginning of a long-standing professional relationship and a great friendship.

In mid-February 1979, we met at San Francisco International Airport for the eleven-hour flight to Tokyo. There was no way to be certain when a slaughter might take place. That all depended on when large numbers of dolphins arrived. But by looking at dates of previous roundups, I'd been able to take a calculated risk. And even if we missed getting the damning documentation of the slaughters, we could still tell the story of the predicament of the fishermen.

The following day, when we arrived at the Japan Airlines counter at Haneda Airport for the domestic flight to the southern Japanese city of Fukuoka, Howard, Steve, John and I shuttled our mountain of cameras, film, tripods, underwater cameras, suitcases, and other specialized gear into the terminal. When we reached the check-in counter, we had less than half an hour before our flight was scheduled to depart. The agent behind the counter was a heavy-set young man about five feet ten inches tall. He looked up at my six feet six inches and then at the pile of gear. For just an instant, a look of shock crossed his face, replaced immediately by one of courteous dedication.

"May I see your tickets please. All this is your baggage?" he said in fluent and only slightly accented English.

I nodded that it was and mumbled a few words of Japanese. "*Hai, dozo.*" ("Yes, please take it").

"Your flight is leaving in only twenty-five minutes." By his tone, he was admonishing me for our late arrival, but after noting my lack of response, he leaped into action with an intensity that evoked images of the martial arts.

"I cannot check in all this gear in so short a time. You send all of your men on the next plane. They will carry only their personal effects. Here are their boarding passes. They must go immediately to the gate," he said with no indication there was room for discussion. Looking back at me, he said, "You will stay here. It will cost you too much to send this as excess baggage so we will do it air freight." He ripped a telephone from its cradle and shouted orders into it. From his tone, he could have been ordering troops into battle.

In less than five minutes, four uniformed and helmeted baggage handlers charged into the building and attacked the pile of gear. Thousands of dollars' worth of equipment disappeared into the back of a Datsun pickup truck, for which the baggage handlers gave me a piece of paper covered with handwritten Japanese characters. I was six thousand miles from home in a strange airport. Our gear was gone, my crew was headed for a remote island without me, and all I had was an unintelligible receipt to show for it. "But this is Japan," I told myself. "There is nothing to worry about."

I was on the next flight to Fukuoka, where I met the rest of the crew. We took a small plane to Iki. The gear was waiting for us when we entered the tiny terminal.

By nightfall We were settling into a *ryokan*, or country inn, on the harbor in Katsumoto town. The floors were covered with tatami, woven rice straw mats; the walls nothing more than *shoji* paper. Ornamental vases and flowers showed the attention and love of the proprietors for their inn. Neither of them was more than five feet tall, and we must have appeared as barbarian giants as we entered the inn. Nevertheless, they were wonderfully polite and accommodating to a scruffy band of foreign travelers. They got us into baths quickly and then handed us yukatas, a male version of the kimono.

They prepared a Japanese feast for our dinner. We had not lost track of our mission but could not escape the growing paradox that, while here to expose the brutality of the fishermen of this very town, we were falling in love with Japan and its people.

Before going to bed, I walked along a harbor as filled with the small, white fiberglass fishing boats as Tokyo's Ginza district is packed with vehicles at rush hour. The weather was surprisingly pleasant for February: clear skies and temperatures in the high sixties. The last fishermen to return at the end of the day were unloading their catch and chatting at quayside. They appeared tired but happy.

Across the inlet leading to the open sea was a small island covered with wind-worn pine trees: Tatsunoshima. That's where they kill the dolphins.

The fishermen suggested that we go to Tatsunoshima Island to film the monument they had erected to the souls of the dolphins they'd killed. They seemed to feel that if we understood they respected the souls of those dolphins, we might be less antagonistic to their deeds.

The cooperative provided an outboard motor boat to ferry us across the mile of water that separates Katsumoto Town from Tatsunoshima. As we came ashore at a small wooden dock, several bottlenose dolphins and two pseudorca lay dead in the shallow water, their stomachs slit from the neck to the anus, entrails washing in the current. The bodies showed no evidence of decomposition, so the slaughter must have happened only a few days before. We had come too late to save these dolphins or even to film their slaughter.

We found the stone monument six feet in height with Japanese characters written in gold. As Knoop set up to film, I walked farther down the beach and stopped to imagine what must have happened here only days before. As I stood there, I began to sink into the sand. I looked down at my feet. Viscous red oozed up around my boots, puddling in the impressions made by my weight on the sand. I stood frozen in horror. The sand was literally saturated with the blood of hundreds, maybe thousands, of dolphins killed and buried there in shallow sand graves. This year, there would be no photograph to alert the world, nothing to even acknowledge the event, except for the ghastly evidence congealing around my feet.

I was sinking into the burial pit of whole tribes of dolphins: mothers, fathers, babies, brothers, sisters, and friends sharing a common hole in the ground, still leaking the dark red blood which had only recently fueled their lives. I stood helpless, searching my mind first to grasp what had happened, then for a way to undo what had been done; to divine a means to reverse hard reality and somehow resurrect these creatures to swim back to the world in which they belonged. But they were dead forever. The only thing now was to stop it from happening again.

We sought a meeting with leaders of the fishermen's union and were ushered into a cold, damp room to meet officials of the Katsumoto Fishermen's Cooperative. Mr. Obata, president of the organization, gave an order, and someone plugged in a space heater to take the chill out of the air. The steaming hot *cha* he offered did the job better than the heater. We set up the cameras and sound gear to film the conversation.

Obata and his colleagues listened politely as I spoke through an interpreter, explaining our concern for the dolphins. I told them of the extraordinary intelligence and sophisticated communications abilities of dolphins. I suggested that the decline in the fish catch might be the result of larger environmental factors unrelated to dolphins—overfishing and pollution in the breeding areas. The Japanese remained impassive, nodding only occasionally so as not to appear impolite. The union officials then took a turn and told us they regretted the need to kill the dolphins and pointed out with great significance they had built a shrine to the souls of those they had been forced to kill.

It quickly became clear they were not terribly impressed with the ideas their visitors were offering, but they seemed to have a healthy respect for the cameras we had brought—perhaps thinking of last year's photo of dead dolphins that had now brought a foreign film crew to their door step. They asked me what kind of film I was making, and I told them I wanted to portray their side of the story as well as represent the animal rights point of view. They feigned nonchalance as then asked me what I would do with the film, and looked at one another with concern when I said the film would be seen around the world. They had no way to know how little certainty there was in that boast.

Still, the union leaders spoke with conviction that once they explained their predicament to us we would gain a fuller understanding of reality and go home. "The dolphins are eating all our fish. Our livelihood is in jeopardy. We must kill the dolphins. Last year, we invited the press to see all the dead dolphins to know the terrible problem we have with the 'sea pigs' [as they call dolphins], but foreigners have seized the picture and turned it against us. They do not understand our livelihood is at stake."

Over and over we heard the word *livelihood*. The crowning irony came when they told us earnestly that they had called in the press themselves and had shown them the massacre! I imagined that over the past year, they had found another public relations firm. It was disturbing to think that if they hadn't publicized the event themselves, the killing would have gone on completely unnoticed and we certainly wouldn't have been sitting there that day.

When it became clear that we foreigners would be slow to be enlightened, the union officials agreed to rent us a boat.

The following morning, we boarded a speedy patrol boat and headed out of port at sun up for the fishing area. We were told the boat we were on is normally used to police the Shichiriga Banks to make sure fishermen from other parts of Japan or even Korea don't come here. They weren't worried solely about dolphins plundering "their" resource.

The number of fishing boats on the Shichiriga Banks, fourteen miles from Iki Island, was astonishing. Hundreds of boats, each with a CB radio crackling, ran back and forth, with one or two fishing lines dangling from its side. When the captain of the union boat carrying us saw a nearby fisherman land a yellowtail, he could not resist. He grabbed a hand line and dropped a hook over the side. Before long, he was hauling the line back in screaming, "*Buri-buri! Buri-buri,*" the Japanese word for yellowtail, as he pulled a shining silver fish about twenty inches long over the gunwales.

The delirious smile on this fisherman's face told the story of what was happening at Iki. The fish was worth about fifty dollars, and far more than that in personal terms. In catching the fish, this man had just thrown a touchdown pass. This was his thing, his profession, his way of keeping points in the game of life. For this fisherman, to catch a yellowtail was winning. And the dolphins threatened to make him a loser.

But the decline of the coastal fisheries was not the immediate financial disaster that it might have at first appeared. While the catch declined, the value of each fish, conforming to the laws of supply and demand, increased. This was especially true because all around Japan, fishing grounds were being exhausted. The increase in price sustained the fishing industry and allowed the men of Iki to continue fishing the last of the stocks. A single yellowtail, once worth a couple of dollars, was now worth fifty (in 1979 dollars), so a day when only a dozen fish were caught was still considered successful.

From the number of boats working the Shichiriga banks it was obvious there was serious over-fishing taking place. The fishermen themselves lamented this. As Japan industrialized, an increase in pollutants in the breeding grounds was destroying the fish eggs before they could mature. But the fishermen could do nothing about these powerful forces. They believed their only recourse was to kill off the dolphins they saw as competition for the diminishing resources.

We returned to port under a cobalt blue sky with the setting sun casting a golden sheen over the seascape. We'd seen masses of fishing boats but no dolphins. I felt strangely at home on this ship in far off waters. Maybe the magic light of late afternoon cast its beneficence over the internal, as well as the external, world. That evening we shared another magnificent meal at the *ryokan*. The conversation was all about how much we loved the people, the village, and the food.

The following morning we set out again - this time as a guest of one of the fishermen. At the dock we met our host for the day, Mr. Harada Susumu, president of the young fishermen's cooperative. Harada was a handsome man, of medium height by American standards, in his late twenties, dressed in a blue Adidas running suit with crew-cut hair. He smiled broadly at us, bowing politely as we approached. As we began loading gear on his boat, our translator warned us that the fishermen were probably inviting us out with the expectation that once we saw what was happening in the fishing area and learned the truth of their predicament, we would drop this dolphin-saving nonsense and go home.

Harada-san's boat was sleek white fiberglass, about thirty feet long, with a small cabin and a powerful engine that got us off the dock and out into the channel quickly. Once in the inlet between Katsumoto and Tatsunoshima, we joined dozens of other fishing boats running full throttle past the breakwater toward the Shichiriga Banks. These guys were not only racing to be first to the fishing grounds, they were also drag racing one another, playing chicken as they approached the narrows at the harbor entrance. The day was bright and clear, the temperature in the mid-sixties.

We cruised smoothly for forty minutes, and despite our grim mission, I reveled in the feeling of being in new waters, in the Straits of Tsushima at the mouth of the Sea of Japan. We were just a few miles from Pusan, Korea. From cliffs, Iki islanders could have seen the historic battle of the Straits of Tsushima, where the Imperial Japanese navy had destroyed the navy of the Russian tsar in 1905.

Less than an hour out of port, small white boats became visible in the distance. They appeared as a solid white line across the horizon until we approached close enough to distinguish individual boats, all very much like Harada's. Everywhere there were boats, boats, boats across the entire Shichiriga Banks. The cacophony from the CB radios and the roar of engines made the scene feel like the beginning of a stock car race. As he cut the wheel to move through the swarm of his fellow fishermen, we set up the camera and began to interview Mr. Harada.

"When I graduated from high school there were so many squid, they were like trash," he said through our interpreter. "These days the fish have become very few, and I really think it is the fault of the dolphins. We now bring in only 10 percent of what we caught eight years ago."

I spoke to him of the relationship we had with the spotted dolphins in the Bahamas, of their brain size, and of my conviction that they were as sentient as we were. Finally Harada Susumu admitted he was sorry they needed to kill dolphins and emphasized, in an almost pleading tone, that the fishermen did not intend to wipe dolphins out entirely. They only wanted to control their numbers. He kept looking at me for some sign that I understood his plight. When I looked out at all the boats buzzing around us, he knew what I was thinking and lowered his eyes. Killing dolphins was something the fishermen could do. Controlling the number of humans, their neighbors and fellow islanders, exploiting the resources on Iki was beyond their means or will.

And, of course, the Iki Islanders were not unique in wanting to destroy competition for what they considered "their resources". In the United States, we had placed bounties on wolves and nearly exterminated them. Sea otters are blamed for ravaging abalone, seals for eating depleted salmon stocks, and in Norway, killer whales for taking too many herring.

Now in the middle of the banks, Harada cut the engine and the boat lost way, but he didn't drop anchor. As the boat drifted and bobbed in the swells, Harada and his brother quickly had their gear in the water and almost immediately brought in a pair of yellowtail and even a squid. The squid was cut up and offered to us as sashimi with a little soy and green Wasabi sauce so fiery hot that it sent a jolt of pain into my skull. Catching any fish was cause for excitement. We quickly found that we were enjoying ourselves with Mr. Harada. It felt like a camaraderie had begun to develop between the Japanese and the foreigners.

As much as I liked Harada, and as much as we seemed to have rapport on a personal level, the day was discouraging. It was becoming clear that he was absolutely unable to project compassion beyond his own family, village, and nation, certainly not beyond his own species. He could not even imagine the existence of a dolphin universe—a place where creatures different from, but no less than he, create a reality as genuine as his own; a space where such creatures live and perceive and feel as intensely and as truly as he. Nor would he project onto himself the agonies of this other creature as it was driven into a bay and then waited for its own death while hearing its family and pod mates cry out in terror. In the end, it was clear that he understood what we said and that we understood what he said, but both parties came to different conclusions about the same information. And of course, our interests were different. That is always the key.

Harada Susumu is an intelligent, energetic, bright-spirited, hospitable person who loves his family—the kind of man you would value as a friend. And he killed dolphins. For him, as for virtually all of us, immediate threats take precedence over longer-term threats and certainly over abstract argument. I knew that if we couldn't make progress with Harada, we would make none with the other islanders.

The following day a huge storm moved in from Siberia, shutting down fishing. Huge, frothing walls of water swept through the harbor at Katsumoto and smashed against the jetties in slow-motion explosions of foam. Rain slashed from skies as gray as the slate roofs of the town buildings. Sitting in the inn, staring out over the rounded tile roofs of the village, I realized that we weren't getting a movie, at least not the movie we'd come for. We had still not seen a single living dolphin, nor the dolphin drive and killing. I worried about the investors and could hear the meter ticking. Each day cost more than $2,000 (in 1979 money) to maintain us in the field and pay the crew. I was discouraged that we hadn't been able to film the fishermen's interactions with the dolphins, only the grotesque aftermath. There was no way to know when or even if another migration of dolphins would pass through the waters off Iki. The fishermen knew as little about that as we did.

"God," I thought, "I've asked investors for money, brought a film crew halfway around the world, and we can't even find a dolphin. And what makes me think I can influence these fishermen anyway?" It looked as though the storm would last for several more days so I decided to bail out, get everyone on a plane home as soon as possible, and cut our financial losses.

As we piled our gear into a van, we imagined the owners of the *ryokan*, whose hotel we had disturbed with our loud *gaijin* comings and goings and our heavy gear, were glad to see us leave, though we never felt a hint of resentment or discourtesy from them. And I supposed that Mr. Harada thought we would be a onetime occurrence in his life, curiosities, maybe a little threatening but now gone. I hoped that the friendly atmosphere that had grown between him and our group would provide the basis for future progress in solving both the threat to the dolphins and the threat to the fishermen's way of life. But one thing of which there was no doubt—I would be back.

I wrote a script for a film based on our visit to Iki and then turned the footage over to Ron Blau, a highly competent editor in Cambridge, Massachusetts. Three months later, a thirty-minute film called *Island at the Edge* came out of his editing room. It told the story as I had experienced it, and in a way I hoped would help save both the lives of the dolphins and the livelihood of the fishermen. By now, the two were inextricably linked for me.

This was the first film I had ever produced on my own though I'd done many short news pieces for CBS News and had co-produced *Dolphin*. The story it told was simple. The fishermen of Iki are hardworking family people. They are energetic, courteous, good humored, and friendly. Fishing is their livelihood, their sport, their measure of themselves. But overfishing and pollution of the coastal waters of Japan have caused the collapse of fishing around Japan, and now both fishermen and dolphins are converging on one of the last productive fishing areas. As in countless cases throughout history, a conflict over resources has led to a war, and here, one side has all the weapons. The film ended by suggesting the solution for the fishermen is not to kill dolphins, but to restore the abundance of the ecosystem.

While done in a documentary style, *Island at the Edge* was a very personal film. It reflected the fact that I'd grown to admire the very people who kill dolphins while deploring the fact that they do it. And I felt that depicting that contradiction in the film raised the story of the dolphin murder at Iki from simplistic propaganda to a true description of why wildlife and wilderness are being destroyed all over the world. Environmentalists lambasted me for showing sympathy for the dolphin-killing fishermen. They suggested that I ought to have used more footage of dead dolphins to raise hatred against Japan and that I should portray the islanders as inhuman butchers. But I was proud of the film because I thought it told the truth, and if the truth were told fully, it would contribute both to ending dolphin killing and greater understanding between adversarial forces.

Island at the Edge won best documentary at the San Francisco International Film Festival but was not widely seen. It was a complicated film and found little success in the market place. Environmentalists didn't support it because it did not portray abject evil. PBS wouldn't touch it because, as one programmer explained, "We need upbeat wildlife films for pledging purposes. Dead dolphins will turn our viewers off."

I looked forward to returning to Iki the following year to screen *Island at the Edge* to the fishermen and continue our effort to find a genuine solution to the problem of declining fish catches at Iki and around Japan. But that was not the way things turned out. When I planned the return trip to Japan, I had in mind shooting a film that would cover what I expected would be a breakthrough between the dolphin lovers and the fishermen of Iki. I had far less money than the previous year, so Howard Hall and I comprised the entire crew.

I worked out a promotional deal with Pan Am that exchanged a credit in the forthcoming film for two first-class roundtrip tickets to Osaka. We departed San Francisco International Airport in late January 1980. En route, Howard and I feasted on caviar and cracked crab on ice while throwing down a fair number of vodka shooters. I don't remember the end of the flight very well. But I do remember that Howard revealed that he'd just had his left arm and ribs broken by a gray whale in San Ignacio Lagoon, Mexico. The whale had hit him with its tail fluke while Howard was filming a mating group in near zero visibility water. The fact that he was on a plane with me headed for Iki only a week after the injury tells you a lot about the courage and tenacity of this guy.

We woke up our first morning in Osaka and saw a story on the front page of the *Japan Times,* an English-language paper published in Japan. The story's headline reported "200 Rare Whales Captured at Taiji." The animals were melon-headed whales, actually a species of dolphin. The story went on to say that the dolphins would be killed to provide food for lions at the Shirahama Zoo. It struck me as extraordinarily perverse that these magnificent wild dolphins would be killed to feed captive lions.

We changed plans on the spot and headed for Taiji, a small village of some thirty-five hundred people on the coast east of Osaka. We arrived in Taiji, found accommodations in a hotel, and walked out to the small bay where the pitiful dolphins were being held. The coast there is magnificent with endless bays and coves formed at the juncture of mountains and sea, making the horror of the scene even more poignant.

Our presence disturbed the fishermen who had driven the dolphins into the bay. They were aware of the international outrage provoked by the slaughter at Iki the year before and didn't welcome foreign observers—especially those with cameras. There wasn't much Howard and I could do directly, so we just hung around the bay with our still and movie cameras at hand. The fishermen seemed stymied. They held meetings. Two days passed. Some of the dolphins succumbed

Author in futile attempt to aid melon-head dieing of shock.

© Howard Hall 1980

Author observes melon-head fetus aborted due to stress of capture at Taiji.

© Howard Hall 1980

and sank into the depths of the cove, but most remained alive. Howard and I worried that while the fishermen were talking, the dolphins weren't eating and might starve. In addition, dolphins don't drink and depend entirely for their hydration on the fish they eat.

Almost more poignant than the plight of the melon-heads – at least their tribe was intact – was that of an adult and juvenile bottlenose dolphin. In the area of Hatajiri Bay now known as The Cove, a half dozen bottlenose dolphins were being held in small net pens. The bottlenose pair, which I assumed to be a mother and calf, remained just outside the nets cruising back and forth, day after day. They were not constrained by any form of net. The stayed of their own volition, held only by their loyalty to and love for one or more of the dolphins in the net pens.

On the third day of captivity for the melon-heads, the fishermen informed us that as a gesture of goodwill, the dolphins would be released. I believe they were afraid of attracting the same kind of international outrage that had been focused on Iki. The following morning, the fishermen drew back the net separating the melon-heads from freedom. But the dolphins didn't budge. Confusion or shock or the knowledge that members of their pod were sick or injured kept the group huddled at the end of the bay farthest from the net.

The fishermen brought a small skiff driven by an outboard motor in behind the dolphins and began revving the engine. The dolphins started to move. The skiff herded them until they were past the net line. Once out of confinement with a clear vision of open ocean ahead, the whole pod erupted into spectacular porpoising leaps across the face of the sea. I remained poker faced, but inside, I was wild with joy. Maybe our cameras were all powerful.

But we could not free the imprisoned bottlenose dolphins in the net pens nor end the anguish of the two bottlenose who had not been selected for a life in captivity but were losing their loved ones.

A day and a half later, we arrived at Iki, still exuberant at our success. We fully believed that the sympathetic treatment we'd given the fishermen in my film *Island at the Edge* and the rapport established the previous year might lead to a similar success here. On the boat from the main island to Iki, we met Dexter Cate, an old Greenpeace campaigner, and his wife, Susie, carrying their infant son. Dexter always presented a warm smile as though something inside him saw beyond quotidian life. He wore his hair to below his shoulders with a bandana to keep it in place, cutting a rakish figure.

Once on the island, reality reared its ugly head when we discovered the *ryokan* of the previous year would not accept us. "We are full," they claimed, but an interpreter who had come with Dexter told us they did not want to be associated with the *gaigin* in the minds of their fellow villagers. We found another inn farther down the docks. They probably didn't want us either but welcomed the business.

I was anxious to find Harada and set off with an interpreter along the Katsumoto town waterfront. The number of boats in the harbor seemed to have increased, if such a thing were possible. Boats were tied to the sterns of other boats tied to the wharf.

We found Harada-san standing with a group of a dozen fellow fishermen. When he saw us, his eyes dropped sharply. He tried to disappear into a group of men. I didn't get it, walked over, and peered down into the midst of the fishermen from the additional foot in height I have over them. Harada finally emerged from the group with a very sheepish smile on his face. We spoke briefly through the interpreter. He was extremely reticent at my suggestions that we head out to sea together during the coming days. His behavior was baffling.

Looking across the straits between Katsumoto and Tatsunoshima, we could see the water's surface strangely agitated. Then the familiar glint of sunlight on a cetacean back told us why Harada was so uncomfortable. Hundreds of dolphins were trapped over there, and the fishermen intended to kill them.

Eight hundred bottlenose and Risso's dolphins had been herded into the bay at Tatsunoshima. We tried to find a boat to carry us across the straits, but no one would oblige. The town had closed ranks against us. But walking around town nosing into things, our interpreter found an old man who hadn't gotten the word. For a few yen, he was glad to carry us across to look at the pretty islands. He told us with great delight, "They have captured many dolphins. They eat all our fish, so we must kill them. That should be very interesting for you."

We did not go directly toward the netted-off bay where the dolphins were being held. Instead, we landed around a point of land separated from the capture area by a steep, tree-covered hill. Our landing party was composed of Howard and myself, Dexter, Susie, and their son—not exactly a Navy SEAL team. Howard and I slung the camera gear over our shoulders and began climbing the hill. The dry, rocky hillside gave under our feet, and we slipped back down the escarpment several times, trying to protect the gear even more than our bodies. After half an hour of climbing and beating our way through bushes, we were on the descent side facing the bay. But the trees still in front of us were high enough that we couldn't see what was happening below.

When we reached the bottom of the hill, Howard and I crawled through a gully toward the beach. We crouched behind a stand of bushes and looked out across the bay upon a sight that will remain forever seared into my memory. The water was boiling with great flaming crimson splashes that looked like the explosions of depth charges. Two hundred yards across the bay, they were killing dolphins. Howard pointed immediately below us at dozens of bottlenose dolphins beached by the outgoing tide, many of them still alive. We began filming. It's all you can do in a moment like this—record it so the world will know, so the deaths of these dolphins will not have been entirely unnoticed and meaningless. Filming is also a way of suppressing emotions. The world through a camera lens is unreal enough that some cameramen have unblinkingly filmed their own deaths.

Suddenly Howard stood up.

"For Christ's sake, get down," I yelled at him. Oddly, he was smiling. "What are you trying to do?" I beseeched him.

"The game's up, Hardy. They've found us."

Walking toward us were two islanders, short, middle-aged men in parkas and windbreakers. One had a scarf across his face. At that moment, a helicopter from a major Japanese news organization buzzed across the bay twisting and turning to give their cameraman the angles he needed to cover this event.

The fishermen shouted at us in Japanese, but we had no translator so we didn't understand a word. "*Wakarimasen*," is all I could say, meaning "I do not understand."

In order to get more film and photographs, I feigned interest in what the fishermen were doing and we all walked along the beach strewn with the bodies of dead and dying dolphins. Theirs were not quick deaths. Their internal organs are crushed by their own weight out of water, and their skin cracked in the heat of the sun. I looked into the eyes of one dying dolphin after another. There was an almost unbearable frustration at being utterly unable to do anything for them.

The fishermen kept talking and trying to lead us around the bay to their main group. I wasn't entirely sure I wanted to be in the midst of all those men carrying spears and in a very killing mood. As we walked, the fishermen stepped on the bodies of the still-living dolphins as though they were rocks. The dying dolphins let out piercing cries that tore at my guts. Those men had absolutely no idea of what they were doing, no comprehension that they were dealing with living, thinking, sentient creatures. I tried to make allowances for the fishermen's ignorance, but my well of forgiveness for these people had run dry. What they were doing was criminal, brutal, insensitive, and self-serving. In my mind it was mass murder.

The fishermen insisted that we follow them around the bay, and finally after scrambling over rocks and walking along the beach at the base of the bay, we stood before blood-caked dolphins stacked in piles. Many were dead. Others, still living, thrashed, whipping the bloody sand with their last convulsive efforts to stay alive in a situation that was utterly incomprehensible to them.

The air was filled with high-pitched dolphin distress calls. A fisherman would flip aside a cigarette and casually wade into the water to grab a dolphin and tie a rope around its tail. A gang of a dozen or so men would grab the other end of the line and pull the dolphin from the water, bouncing onto the pile of its comrades already dead or dying on the beach. Finally, another fisherman plunged his spear into the dolphin's side. The fishermen's idea of compassion was to stab the dolphin in the carotid artery so it would bleed out quickly.

For a moment, Howard and I were in shock. My mind struggled to find something we could do to stop the killing, but there was nothing. There were dozens of men. Some were killing. Others stood around eating lunch. Many of them had spears and knives and looked at us with anger and confusion.

When we started to photograph the dreadful scene, a man with a spear approached us and started yelling. "*Wakarimasen,*" I smiled at him. He scowled in confusion. He had no idea what to do. We knew they wanted to kill us, but something held them back.

Dexter and Susie arrived, their son on Dexter's shoulders. The fishermen looked at the child in a genuinely friendly fashion. Children, they value. Dolphins, they do not. They offered us sake and pieces of fish and rice. Another fisherman, smiling, proffered a spear, inviting us to join in the sport of killing. We kept making 16-mm movies and 35-mm stills.

When we had been on the beach for half an hour, there was nothing more to film. It was the same scene over and over. Without the activity of filming or a camera lens to peer through, I received the full impact of what was happening in front of me: the tribe from the sea was being reduced to scraps.

As we stood on a small hill overlooking the bloody bay, the interpreter told me we would have been beaten or killed except that the fishermen thought we'd come from the helicopter that was circling overhead when we arrived on Tatsunoshima. If they have a helicopter, the fishermen erroneously concluded, they must be connected to power.

Partly from fear that someone would confiscate the footage and anxious to get the images out to the world, I took the first flight off Iki Island the next morning. In Tokyo, I brought the footage to the CBS News bureau, where they processed and syndicated it by satellite around the world. When it aired internationally, it caused a worldwide tsunami of revulsion and protest.

The power of being on the scene with a camera was not a new concept. Images from Selma had been pivotal in awakening America to the evil and stupidity of segregation. CBS's *Hunger in America* had opened our eyes to the plight of migrant workers. What was different at Iki was that we were not a network camera crew. Howard and I were two guys on a shoestring budget just putting ourselves on the scene hoping to make a huge impact.

An Iki Island fisherman stabs a bottlenose dolphin
© Howard Hall 1980

That night, Dexter paddled from town across to Tatsu-noshima Island in a small inflatable kayak. Throughout the night, he cut nets, hoping to free the dolphins that had not been killed. It was an incredibly brave thing to do. In the morning, suffering severe hypothermia, he sat down and waited to be arrested. He spent six months in jail and was then expelled from Japan and declared *persona non grata* so he could never return. Few, if any, dolphins escaped from the nets. Partly this was due to the unfamiliarity of swimming in shallow water with obstructions all around them. But it also involved the fact that dolphins will not leave their families and pods. But Dexter's trial brought tremendous publicity to the atrocities at Iki that, combined with the gruesome images Howard and I had taken, would mostly end the killing of dolphins at that island.

In the days following broadcast of our footage, more than two hundred reporters showed up at Iki. The villagers were stunned. The lessons learned at Iki about the power of a man with a camera would take on entirely new meaning with the dawn of the Internet.

~ 4 ~

I See that You See Me

I had no way to know this, but seven thousand miles away a young woman was watching CBS News in her dorm at the University of Minnesota. The footage Howard Hall and I had shot at Iki originated from the CBS News bureau in Tokyo, bounced off a satellite, picked up a narration track at CBS News in New York where I had worked through the early seventies, and appeared on her television screen as she was dressing for school. As a person who loves animals, she was appalled and revolted at the sight of the dolphin massacre.

In the spring of 1980, after I returned to the United States from Iki, I appeared on the *Today Show* with Tom Brokaw and on local news. Day after day, I fed stills and film clips to media around the world. The ghastly images of dolphins thrashing in blood red water were never far from my waking consciousness and kept me awake late into the night. But I vowed their deaths would not go unnoticed and unavenged.

I was frantic to get back to the Bahamas to continue shooting a second film on the spotters, convinced the world needed to see the social lives and intelligence of dolphins. But I didn't have a budget for a film. In those days, there were few outlets for wildlife documentaries on national television.

To fund my filming, I set up a charter for June of 1980 on a sailboat sleeping eight people, and sold berths on the boat to cover the costs. By this time, I had purchased a 16-mm camera in a small housing and was ready to do my own shooting. Hiring cameramen was just too expensive.

But before the trip to the Bahamas, I received an invitation to spend a week aboard *Don Jose*, a motor craft that carried tourists in the Sea of Cortez. I was exhausted when I arrived at the ship and slept a good part of the way from San Felipe to the Canal de las Ballenas where fin whales are found year around.

Toward the end of day two, we came upon a small group of finbacks feeding in a glassy sea. My first awareness of them came as a ghastly stench. I heard an explosion and was assaulted by an overpowering odor. "My God, the toilet has exploded," I thought. In fact, the sound and odor were the exhalation of a finback right under our bow. We stayed with the whales for several hours steering to position ourselves upwind of them.

I woke up the morning of day three to find *Don Jose* anchored in fog just off an utterly barren island covered with birds. Thousands of Heermann's gulls, and royal and elegant terns occupied every square yard of the sand and guano covered islet called Isla Raza

The captain announced we would be going ashore.

"Why in hell would we want to go see birds when there are whales and dolphins around?" I thought.

But I went with the group, wearing a T- shirt branded with the ABC American Sportsman logo. I was pretty proud of that shirt, which had been given to me when I did a shoot for them off Maui. A bird shat on it immediately. Pride goeth before the fall.

I got separated from the rest of the passengers and was kneeling at the water's edge trying to get a photograph of an oystercatcher. Two sneaker-shod feet appeared beside me. I raised my head. Long, deeply tanned legs were topped by a pair of very short shorts. Farther up, a pretty, young woman with face burned deep bronze and hair almost to her waist was staring disapprovingly at me.

"You're off the clearly marked paths," she said. "If you step on an egg, you'll destroy two birds' investment in their next generation."

"Uh, sorry."

I followed her back to the path demarcated by stones dabbed with white paint and then kept following her. I thought, "This is quite a woman. Too bad I'll never see her again." I gazed in awe at the tens of thousands of birds nesting in the valleys of the island and then jumped back onto a panga and was shuttled back to *Don Jose*.

But when *Don Jose* pulled anchor Julia Whitty, the young woman who had put me on the right path, was aboard to do a bird census. We spent hours talking on the deck in front of the bridge as we ran north along the eastern side of Isla Angel de la Guarda. She disagreed with me on a lot of things and could hold her ground. I was accustomed to women pretty much agreeing with me, so her keen intelligence really caught my attention.

There's a sound in the original film *War of the Worlds*, a kind of *wuuu-ahhhh-wuuuing*. I began to hear that sound as our conversation progressed. Not only was she intelligent and knowledgeable, but our discussion turned to World War II, an area of history that had fascinated me since I was six years old. At the same instant, we each started talking about what was probably the greatest tank battle in history that had taken place at Kursk, Russia, in the summer of 1943.

We both came to the realization that something extraordinary was happening. The *wuuu-ahhhh-wuuuing* got louder. When I mentioned that I had shot the film of the dolphin massacre at Iki her cool demeanor evaporated and she said, "*You* were the one who shot that footage!"

We were married four months later and worked as partners in the dolphin research and filmmaking. She brought the scientific expertise, and I had the journalistic experience.

Julia was finishing her work on Raza Island so was not on the 1980 trip to White Sand Ridge. But beginning in 1981, she accompanied me on every expedition for ten years as we pieced together a sequel to the first dolphin film.

In June 1980, I left West End on *Sir Cloudesley Shovell*, a sixty-five-foot gaff-rigged schooner, captained by a quintessential Brit named Bob Gascoine. Looking back I'm amazed I stuck to my dream of making this film on dolphins.

The year before, 1979, had been a disaster. The captain we hired wouldn't go far enough north to reach the dolphin grounds and eventually just hauled us one hundred miles south to Bimini, where he could go ashore and drink. We had absolutely no contact with the spotted dolphins.

On the 1980 expedition, Howard Hall was along as cameraman, and I was doing some shooting myself. Steve Gagne didn't bring his "underwater piano" but did have a hydrophone and underwater amp. We found the dolphins about thirty miles north of Grand Bahama and had frequent encounters during the week we were out there.

On our first entry into the water, dolphins swarmed around us for a couple of minutes, then left to be replaced by a single male who charged at Howard and me. His eyes were blazing red, a sign of excitement and probably aggression. He was using his sonar intensely, and I thought to myself, "This guy's not pleased to see us."

After several passes, he just drifted off. My guess is he figured he'd discharged his duty by determining we were too slow and stupid to be of any harm to the rest of the school. We named him Big Eye. Of course, the wide eyes might have been only an indicator of his state of mind, but we didn't know that at the time.

A trio of dolphins became the first we were able to identify in a way that would be valid for years to come. Spotted dolphins are born solid pearly gray. They develop spots as they mature so a spotting pattern that is noted one year is useless the next. But each member of this group of three dolphins had an immutable body mark. A very young male had a blunt trailing edge to his dorsal fin. We called him Chopper. Another youngster had a rounded left tip to his fluke, so we named him Stubby. The largest of the three was a not fully mature female with substantial spotting. While she had no distinguishing irregularities on her body, she did have a remora, or sucker fish, about fourteen inches long attached to her side.

Remarkably, the remora stuck with her or to her year after year. The presence of this fish made her recognizable for the next five summers. An extraordinarily friendly dolphin, she would swim at us making an up-down whistle while streaming bubbles from her blowhole. This was her signature whistle, or greeting call. Based on the pattern of her call, we named her Didi.

Always feeling a little clumsy and even stupid around the dolphins, I decided to do something that would mystify or at least intrigue them. I dived to the bottom fifteen feet below the boat and sat on the white sand. When Didi and her gang approached, I took off my fin and dropped it in front of them. Didi circled and sonared the fin intensely. Did she think I had pulled off part of my body? In reality, probably not. Her sophisticated sonar could easily distinguish living tissue from the rubber of the fin. Nevertheless, she must have done a little puzzling, and I liked that thought.

The senior males, who traveled in a coalition, would occasionally blast us with investigative sonar. The sound was so intense it resonated in my sternum and sinuses.

When Steve played his clarinet through the underwater amplifying and recording system something remarkable happened. On playback of the recordings, we learned that the dolphins were mimicking the music. They were responding to our "vocal" output. The implications of their mimicking us and displaying their boundless curiosity were enormous. Unfortunately, we had less than two weeks on the banks, and I left feeling frustrated.

The discovery of their efforts to mimic us in 1980 emboldened me to make a full push the following year. I chartered *Tropic Bird* out of St. Thomas in the Virgin Islands for five full weeks at a cost of fifty thousand dollars, vastly more expensive than *Cloudesley*. But she provided quarters for more than twenty passengers, so we were able to accommodate enough paying volunteers to defray the costs. I broke the season into five trips of six days each, originating in West Palm Beach, Florida, sixty miles across the Gulf Stream from the White Sand Ridge.

The paying passengers were signed on as volunteers who would supposedly follow individual dolphins and record their interactions with other members of the pod. And they had the opportunity to watch the production of a unique film about dolphins.

Laden with fifteen cases of photographic and dive gear Howard, Steve, Julia, and I landed in the oppressively thick heat and humidity of south Florida in June. We found our vessel tied to the end of a dock at the harbor. She was a formidable metal ship, nearly one hundred feet long, with a blue hull and white decks. As I stepped aboard her, she was solid under foot, a truly stable vessel with large and powerful engines and the appearance of being shipshape.

Tropic Bird's skipper, another captain named Mike, was a different matter. Dressed in greasy bathing trunks and with his hair matted against his head by engine oil, he resembled many of the engine room derelicts I'd run across during my years of diving. Other members of the crew included Mark, a refugee from advertising and radio work; Meta, a tall, shy girl from New York who seemed a bit too refined for this ship; and Inga, a hefty blonde and very German cook.

Tropic Bird was a former World War II German E boat, something like an American PT boat but built of metal rather than plywood. Captain Mike was very proud of her. He showed us a small dent on the front of his ship and told us she'd acquired this blemish when arriving at a cement dock with too full a head of steam. Unable to stop, *Tropic Bird* had plowed into the dock and demolished it, coming away only slightly dinged herself. While we were impressed with the ship's sturdiness, the story did not entirely contribute to a sense of confidence in its captain.

Our sense of wonderment at Captain Mike grew further when he appeared that evening at dinner wearing a German naval officer's cap with a swastika emblem and a blue and gold uniform coat, several sizes too large for him and hanging to his knees. The sight of his greasy, skinny legs protruding beneath the officer's jacket as he snapped a mock Nazi salute would not have pleased the Führer.

Quite a few ships had been pirated in the waters of the northern Bahamas during recent years. Their owners and crews had been murdered and the hijacked boats used to smuggle drugs into Florida. Mike said that if any pirates tried to take *Tropic Bird* we'd all just go inside and close the hatches. Nothing short of a direct hit from a cannon shell could harm this ex-Nazi ship of war.

To enter the interior of *Tropic Bird*, you had to pull open the huge waterproof (and, Mike assured us, bulletproof) metal door to the main salon. A passage ran forward to what is sometimes over-elegantly called on dive boats an *apres-dive* bar. Steve took over this area as his audio lab, filling it with a Korg synthesizer and keyboard, recorders, hydrophones, and other paraphernalia. Julia set up a system that would allow film crew and volunteers to identify individual spotted dolphins and plot their associations and interactions with fellow pod members. Howard was able to get a corner for his underwater camera systems. We had high-end recording devices on loan from Hubbs-SeaWorld Research Institute, headquartered in San Diego, California, that would allow us to record the dolphins' super–high frequency whistles. The human ear can register up to only 20 kHz, or 20,000 cycles per second. Dolphins can hear up to 150 kHz. While science was not my main purpose, I was glad to be able to produce information that scientists might find useful.

After learning the previous summer that dolphins mimic our sonic output, Steve had gone to work on two new pieces of equipment. The first apparatus would enable us to record dolphin sounds in synchronization with movie film. We felt that if we could film the dolphins and record the sounds they were making at that moment, we could get some insight into how they use both their echolocation and their whistles. The second device, a waterproof, computer-driven synthesizer, had been programmed to replicate, as best a human instrument could do, sounds such as Didi's signature whistle and the heavy click-train barrages we had received from the males. This synthesizer would enable us to reply to the dolphins with sounds they might recognize as mimicking their own vocal output. We hoped this would intrigue them.

It would be hard to overstate the good fortune of meeting Steve, whose enthusiasm, energy, and talent combine with a profound irreverence for ordinary life and a go-for-it attitude. I'm a bit embarrassed that I initially rejected his ideas, thinking him to be just a new-age dreamer.

We crossed the Gulf Stream at night and cleared customs at West End. By early afternoon, we were headed north, the island of Grand Bahama a receding thin line on the southern horizon. That sight never fails to fill me with anticipation. Sandy Cay gave way to Wood Cay, and then land disappeared altogether. I felt the familiar relief of being rid of the world of cars and phones and pressure for a while. But this relief soon gave way to concern about finding the dolphins. I couldn't help but wonder what had happened to Didi, Chopper, Stubby, and the other members of the pod in the year since we'd last seen them. There is no information on the attrition rate for spotted dolphins in the wild, but there was certainly ample evidence that some of them fell victim to sharks. Several of the dolphins known to us had been dinged by sharks but survived the attacks. There was no way to tell how many had been killed.

The Gulf Stream added its force to our forward movement, a gift of two and a half knots, and sooner than expected, we were passing Memory Rock, a quarter mile off our starboard. This signpost, both the last reminder of land and the beginning of dolphin territory, brought the realization of all that was riding on finding dolphins here: three years of effort, all my hopes for making a film, and, most of all, the idea that we could do something to affect the fate of dolphins in the tuna nets and around Iki.

Julia and I chatted on the raised platform just aft of the bow, over the salon where Steve was assembling his gear into something resembling Dr. Frankenstein's lab. I told her again how anxious I was for her to see these incredible creatures, but she retained her scientific reserve, conceding only that she was "sure it will be very interesting."

The usual bureaucratic delay at customs had put us behind schedule, and when it became clear that the sun would reach the horizon before we reached the dolphin grounds, Mike decided to anchor short of our target area. I thought the odds of finding dolphins this far south were low, but getting off the boat seemed a pleasant thing to do. Julia, a couple of the volunteers, and I commandeered the inflatable and headed off, Mark in oil-stained bikini briefs grudgingly at the tiller. It was late in the day, and we were so far from dolphin territory that I didn't even bother to ask Howard to load his camera and give us coverage.

We ran a few hundred yards forward of *Tropic Bird*, which was oriented due east toward the banks. All of us were happy to be skimming over the water in the intensely saturated late-afternoon light. The world seemed completely benign, and we relaxed, basking in the warm, sea-fragrant Bahama breezes. The quality of light was intense, so rich that it was almost oily. During the hours of high sun, the waters here don't reflect light; they soak it up, dampening contrast. But as the filmmaker's "magic hour" arrives in the late afternoon, colors intensify, and the sea seems to radiate back warm, golden light absorbed when the sun was overhead. The towering white cumulus clouds, brilliant against the deepening blue of the sky, made tanned faces appear the more deeply bronzed. There was no visible evidence anyone else existed, nor even that there was such a thing as land.

I was reveling in these sensations when my head snapped to the left. Bursting out of the glassy sea came a phalanx of dolphins headed straight for our bow. The water level view from the inflatable made their appearance immediate and thrilling.

"Dolphins. Spotters. Look at them...coming off the port bow," I was yelling before I knew it.

Julia strained her eyes but saw nothing. The bolting gray forms, distorted as they moved just under the waves, were still unfamiliar to her. The images did not connect with stored experience of past dolphin encounters heralded by just such shifting patterns of rippling light and shadow under the water. Then, with the smallest of splashes, dorsal fins rolled at the surface and concussive *phew* sounds erupted from blowholes like distant gunfire. The dolphins broke the surface under our bow, now plainly visible to everyone, rolling on their sides and looking back into our delighted eyes.

"Stop the boat! Cut the engine!" I yelled as I pulled on my mask and fins. "Am I clear to go in?"

Mark clung to a nonchalance that said, "I've seen all this before. These people are obviously amateurs." He shrugged. "Yeah, sure go for a swim."

I felt a moment of sympathy for him and remembered Herman Melville's words on dolphins in *Moby Dick*: "If you yourself can withstand three cheers at beholding these vivacious fish, then heaven help ye; the spirit of godly gamesomeness is not in ye."

I was over the side and heading for the bottom twenty feet below. Julia swam at my side, and we dived and turned among a dozen dolphins, bellies rosy pink with excitement. I searched the underseascape for Didi, Chopper, and Stubby, but they did not appear. It seemed an insult to hang motionless when the dolphins had issued an invitation to play, so I jackknifed at the waist into a surface dive, propelled myself to the bottom, then turned on my back. I flinched as dolphins shot overhead.

The large adult males swept by, sonaring us vigorously. The vibrations of their echolocation tingled in my skull and spine. If dolphins' sonar can read emotions, they were registering some very heavy exhilaration. Julia and I burst to the surface to yell our discoveries across the twenty yards of glassy water between us. But words could wait for later. She waved a thumbs-up, then buried her face in the water, kicked twice, and rejoined the dolphins underwater. I dived again and saw her wide-eyed with wonder, turning one way then another as the spotters streaked past buzzing and whistling. "What had become of the detached and objective observer?" I laughed into my snorkel. Julia had no lack of "godly gamesomeness."

There were at least twenty dolphins in the pod, divided into several distinct groups. The guardians, composed of six of what we believed were males, maintained a tightly packed cohesion. The sea resonated with clicks and whistles and long, thin lines of bubbles streamed from the blowhole of the leading dolphin in the pack. He appeared to be identifying himself to all around, allowing his pod mates to form up on him in this moment of excitement and possible danger. The guardians presented a formidable appearance. Their formation had a mercurial, shifting aspect, accented by the spotting patterns of the large males. The spotting of the individuals seemed to fuse into a single organism the size of a small whale, making their appearance both intimidating and confusing to any potential predator.

The guardian unit swam to the surface to breathe, then dove and turned toward me. As they approached, they wagged their heads from side to side as they emitted intense click trains of sonar mixed with whistles. When they got to within fifteen feet, they turned to pass me on their side, which allowed them to inspect this improbable visitor with their lively and inquisitive eyes. I could see that in the midst of the adults were some young, unspotted dolphins who had to beat their tails energetically to keep with the formation.

Dolphin affection is common and heart warming

© Howard Hall 1981

Apart from these were groups of three and four dolphins whose spots were just appearing. At this point, we still did not know what part they played in the pod's social structure. And there was a single, totally spotless youngster who charged fearlessly in at the divers, turning his belly toward us as he shot past. From time to time, he would hang in mid-water, sonaring us over and over, clearly trying to decipher what manner of creatures we were.

As the dolphins slid by and headed off on new tangents, our divers began to surface farther and farther apart. Each had been orienting to individual dolphins whose grace and speed compel the eye. Dolphins are always the most alluring element in the barren, and to us, featureless underseascape. As I'd seen in 1978, they quickly become our points of reference, our imagined allies in this shallow but vast ocean.

The sight of divers spread out over such a large area of sea broke the spell for me. I surfaced to see the sun falling fast into the clouds skirting the western horizon, and I knew it was time to gather up. I raised my arm over my head to summon the inflatable. We hauled ourselves aboard without a trace of effort, each face ablaze with excitement, all lips reporting the wonder of the encounter, trying to breathe and talk at the same time.

"They came at me like rockets and turned at the last second."

"Did you see the baby…it wanted to play, but its mother just stuck with it like glue."

The look on Julia's face was not scientific objectivity. It was ecstasy. But a vestige of the scientist remained in her question, "Did you recognize any of them from previous years?" I hadn't, and no one else even waited for answers.

"They're completely unafraid."

"Unbelievable."

"Incredible."

"Fantastic."

I wanted to bring the dolphins back to the boat on the bow of the inflatable so the volunteers could see them, but after covering half the distance, our escorts left us to blend back into the inaccessible recesses of the darkening sea.

In the morning, there were no dolphins in sight, and I asked Mike to run us farther up the banks to the area I thought to be the epicenter of the *Maravilla* dolphins. The volunteers grumbled about leaving this location where we'd just found dolphins, but I was convinced that on the previous evening we'd encountered a school of spotters who swim through the waters just north of Memory Rock on an irregular basis. Since we recognized none of them, I felt certain they were not of the *Maravilla* group.

For the next three days, we cruised the banks with only occasional encounters with bottlenose dolphins who would ride briefly on the bow or ignore us completely. This scarcity of dolphin contact became the breeding ground of theories. Everyone trotted out his or her favorite.

"Something you did last year must have antagonized them."

"They don't like *Tropic Bird*'s motor."

"They're getting tired of humans. The novelty has worn off for them."

One volunteer from Mill Valley, California, had brought aboard crystals, which she'd been arranging in various patterns on the table in the salon. She was certain the dolphins had sensed the "heavy Nazi karma" of our converted German vessel. "You can't get rid of that stuff with a paint brush," she weighed in gravely.

At the end of five days, we had nothing and I was worried. Really worried. It was embarrassing to have brought so many people so far and given them nothing to show for it. At the end of the final day of our first trip, our crew and volunteers were restless and disappointed. One woman was even crying. The crossing back to Florida was rough. We pulled into West

Palm Beach under pewter gray skies with a ship full of seasick passengers.

The second trip did not begin auspiciously. As we headed north after clearing into the Bahamas at West End, we were banging into a six-foot swell. We anchored the first night on the banks behind a shallow reef, the closest thing we could find to shelter. During the night, I tossed and grumbled in my narrow bunk. The bedding was damp with my sweat. "God, that's all we need now—a week of bad weather," I thought.

I ran through the possible reasons for our failure to find dolphins and realized that we might still not be going far enough north on the banks. That shouldn't have been surprising. Boat captains hate these waters. There's no shelter. Each mile north is a mile from safe harbor, taverns, and pretty women, and these shallow banks all look the same to them.

Captain Mike was on watch when I reached the bridge at 4 a.m. I asked him for the Loran coordinates of our current location, and we plotted our position on the map. We were still too far south! We had not yet reached the area where we'd found the dolphins on *Albury* in 1978. I also realized that I'd been assuming the dolphins roamed broadly over a wide area of ocean. Maybe their territory was very tightly focused.

"Mike, tomorrow we head up here," I said indicating the southern dogleg of the upper bank, eight miles north of our current position.

His eyes rolled, but he nodded. "OK."

I left the bridge and brachiated my way through the narrow, heaving passageway back to my bunk. I felt we were down to our last shot.

In the morning, we plowed slowly north through six- to eight-foot swells, the skies covered with dense, rain-laden clouds. The air was warm and humid, and I stood on the bow all morning, joined from time to time by Julia and Howard who were trying to keep up a gallant front. For two hours, there were no dolphins but plenty more theories from the volunteers.

"We'll never find dolphins in this weather. We won't be able to see them in the swells."

"We never find them anyway," I snapped. "They always find us."

The would-have-been German raider smashed an ocean swell and Julia said encouragingly. "It's nice to have a boat that can take the seas. At least we're not uncomfortable."

And then there was a gray shape, a splash just slightly different from the action of wind on wave tops, a shadow moving under a whitecap. A friendly face hurtled off the crest of a massive swell and dived into the trough. The dorsal was blunt at the back. Chopper was flying to our bow. A lightly spotted young adult arrived a dolphin leap behind him. A moment later, there were six and then ten dolphins changing positions with astonishing fluidity each time our bow fell into an oncoming swell, breaking off to take advantage of the stern wake, porpoising forward to nudge another dolphin from its station at the bow. The young adult rolled over to look up at us, revealing the shimmering green remora fish she wore like an outrageous piece of jewelry. I screamed and waved. "Didi!"

Howard saw it too. "There's the one with the remora!"

Julia was skeptical. "Do you really think that after a year, it's the same dolphin?"

I knew from the dolphin's eyes who she was but I wanted more proof. Stubby, Didi's constant companion, arrived, his rounded tail fluke an unmistakable marker.

We yelled and laughed and slapped each other on the back. These were "our" dolphins—not that we owned them but that we recognized them and considered them our friends.

The anchor chain screeched and metal clattered on metal as the links tumbled through a guide slot and splashed through the sea's surface to the sand below. Howard, Steve, Julia, and

I threw on our scuba tanks and weight belts. Short bursts of compressed air punctuated the scramble as we tested regulators. One by one, we flew over the side.

Underwater the world of heaving boats, heavy gear and screaming divers transformed into a light blue-green, gravity-free silence, broken only by the rhythmic, whistling rasp of breathing apparatus. I swam down and waved the bubbles out of my face in time to see Didi, Chopper, and three other dolphins charge straight at me, sonaring and chirping wildly. The female came within inches of my face, turned, circled, and then cranked a series of vertical loops. She seemed to be celebrating the reunion as much as I was.

As she conducted her wide-eyed, intensive sonar inspection, she broadcast her familiar up-down, up-down signature whistle. A thin stream of bubbles trailed almost constantly from her blowhole as she identified herself to us. She swam to within four feet of me, turned sideways to peer into my eyes, then faced straight on to investigate me with a buzz of sonar. I could imagine her saying to herself, "This must be the long one from last year." As she grudgingly broke away to return to the surface to change old air for new, the agitated remora slid over her skin from under her pectoral fin back to the tail, desperately trying to find a secure station in this mayhem.

Several of the dolphins had clearly grown since the previous year. Didi was larger and had more spots. Chopper was no longer a "football," and his first spots were appearing.

Howard was looking left and right, up and down, calculating which of the dolphin groups and formations he should be filming. Didi made up his mind by swimming right in front of his lens. Steve stood on the bottom with his underwater recorder in one hand and his microphone extended at the end of a three-foot pole in the other. Julia swam four feet off the bottom, drawing identification pictures on her white slate with ferocious intensity.

When Didi looked in my direction again, I decided to try to confirm to her that we were the divers she'd encountered the previous summer. I wasn't sure that she'd recognize us since we'd arrived in a different boat, so I took off my fin and dropped it to the white sand bottom. Didi and the other young dolphins swam over and investigated the fin just as they had the previous summer but left it quickly. I picked up the fin, swam up to a depth of fifteen feet over the bottom, and let it drop again. The fin drifted down like a feather. Didi swam by, looked at it, then straight at me, crapped on the fin, and cruised away. Of course, it's possible it was just a random act of defecation, but she was looking at me as she did it, and my distinct impression was that she was deliberately saying, "OK, we see your fin. We know it's you. But now you've got to give us something new."

In our exhilaration, we drained our scuba tanks quickly and returned to the surface. The dolphins faded leisurely into the underwater haze, and we resurfaced into a maelstrom. This was an extremely dangerous situation. We were two hundred yards from the boat. The gravity-bound world of the surface reasserted itself, and our cameras and dive gear weighed us down in the current and six-foot swells that lifted and dropped us as we labored toward *Tropic Bird*. It was too rough to safely deploy the inflatables, so we slowly swam the two hundred yards back to the boat, sharing observations while gasping in air and spitting out water. Julia showed me her drawings as we bobbed up and down past each other. It was like trying to carry on a conversation across a seesaw where one party, then the other is underwater. The remora on Didi's sketch on the slate was obvious, and so were Chopper's and Stubby's body markings.

Once aboard, we dropped our gear on the fantail. We dried off and gathered in the salon to debrief the encounter. Julia had terrific drawings and the presence of Didi and Chopper confirmed we were with the *Maravilla* pod. We continued to speculate about Didi's relationship with the remora; I joked that it might be Didi's pet, and everyone laughed but couldn't be sure I wasn't right. Steve and Howard reported that the sync recording system had worked well, and Steve was particularly pleased with the frequency reducer he had built into his recorder. That little bit of technology brought the frequency of the dolphin ultrasonic vocalizations down into a range humans can easily hear. Through his waterproof headphones, Steve was getting a much richer sample of what the dolphins were saying than the rest of us.

The following morning skies were clear and the swells had dropped. A ten-knot breeze from the southwest kept the heat from becoming oppressive. But there were no dolphins in sight. We ran *Tropic Bird* to see if we could attract them.

Within ten minutes of getting underway, dolphins came from all points of the compass, and soon there were more than a dozen around the boat. Some were riding the bow and others playing in the stern wave. We observed that when the larger, more heavily spotted dolphins took position on the bow wave, they displaced the younger, smaller dolphins. Their broad, heavily spotted backs and the white tips to their beaks made them easy to identify as members of the guardian group. These senior dolphins swim with a dignified, somewhat stiff demeanor, as if aware of their status and responsibilities. We named them "The Heavies," and at that moment, by the act of naming them, we discovered a special affection for this taciturn "band of brothers." The name arose not only because of their larger, more muscled bodies and heavier spotting patterns but also because of the weighty approach this subgroup showed toward life as contrasted with the energy, verve, and innocent curiosity of Didi and the juveniles.

The Heavies had arranged themselves in symmetrical formation just ahead and on either side of the point of the bow, swimming in a formation that resembled the prongs of a fork. They maintained fixed positions throughout their run with us and moved straight ahead with a minimum of motion. When bow riding, they had the aspect of a phalanx. We discussed whether their positions on the bow might reflect individual positions in the hierarchy of the leadership group.

When the Heavies left, Didi and her cohorts would slip in from the side and stern waves and take position on the bow, but they moved fluidly, changing positions constantly, rolling on their backs to swim upside down or onto their sides to look up at us.

From our position looking down on the bow-riding dolphins, we could film slo-mo straight into their blowholes, and this enabled us to calculate the length of time it took for them to breathe. The spotters begin to exhale just under the surface so that when the blowhole rolls clear of the water the lungs are empty and ready to inhale. The inhale, which fills the dolphin's lungs completely, takes eight frames of 16-mm movie film running at standard speed of twenty-four frames per second. Thus, we could calculate that it takes a dolphin one third of a second to completely fill its lungs. Humans normally take perhaps two seconds to fill their lungs only one-fifth of their volume.

After we let the dolphins bow ride for ten minutes, we entered the water to obtain additional identifications. Some of the volunteers took slates and returned good observations, but most were concerned only with getting personal pictures of the dolphins. We realized for the first time that during the hours between 10:00 a.m. and 5:00 p.m., the spotters would rarely approach us, though on very calm days we could see them gathered in small groups just under the surface, resting or playing in a desultory fashion. Toward the end of the day, though, they returned, and late afternoon was generally when we had our best encounters with them.

A key element of our project was to photograph as many individual dolphins as possible and to correlate the development of spotting with age. Chopper would be the most likely candidate for this study since his dorsal fin made him so readily identifiable and we had a pretty good idea of his age from seeing him as a newborn in 1979. We could follow Didi's development as well. We'd filmed her in 1978, though by then she'd already developed spotting so we'd never know more than approximately how old she was. But our best guess was she was about six years old in 1981.

Another of our tasks was to identify the sex of individuals we photographed—no easy task in dolphins. There is sexual dimorphism but it's more subtle than in other animals, at least to creatures such as we who lack the dolphins' "x-ray vision." In the interest of hydrodynamics, and to avoid being a barracuda's dinner, a male's genitals remain inside his body. When ready for use, the bright pink penis switchblades into position. To identify genital slits and mammary openings in females, you need to be within six feet or less of their bellies and the light has to be just right. Later, we learned that males have a taller and straighter dorsal fin, which makes it easier to quickly identify their sex.

The next morning was dead flat and murderously hot. I'd been trying to set a righteous example by staying on dolphin watch while the volunteers cooled themselves in the main salon below watching Clint Eastwood movies. In the brutal heat, the lure of clear, cool water only two decks below became too much. I leaped from the top deck, fifteen feet down into the water, my cannonball producing a satisfying splash. The sound brought others to the top deck, and delight broke out all over. For several minutes, we all jumped, vying to see who could make the biggest dent in the ocean.

Amid this outbreak of frivolity, Captain Mike stuck his head out of the wheelhouse and called out. "If anyone's interested, there are dolphins coming off the port quarter—lots of them."

From the top deck, we could see the Heavies swimming slowly toward us. We grabbed our snorkeling equipment and cameras and swam out to meet them. Perhaps it was the heat of the day, but they seemed calmer than usual, even lethargic, and allowed us to approach them closely and swim alongside them. They didn't seem terribly interested in us, but this was the first chance we'd had to linger among these senior males and a nice opportunity to record identification marks and document their collegial swimming behavior on film.

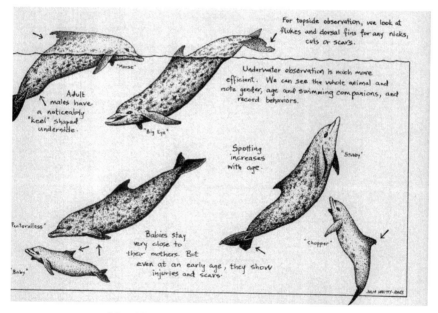

Identification sketches drawn by Julia Whitty summer 1981

From small nicks on their flukes and dorsal, we began to identify and assign names to individual members of the Heavies. We were also able to get close enough to confirm that they were males.

We were beginning to get good data on this pod of friendly dolphins but I wanted more than just biological observations from this unique situation. My greatest hope for capturing something utterly unprecedented on film was the call generator Steve had developed. We were getting useful information and Julia's work in identifying the dolphins was progressing nicely, but the call generator might produce a reaction in the dolphins that would show the world that there are intelligent, thinking, feeling, perhaps even humorous creatures in the ocean. I also hoped that with this device, we'd be able to show the dolphins some sign of our own intelligence and get their reaction to it.

Steve and I decided that when we got in the water, I'd adopt one of the call signs built into the box as my own personal signature whistle. I selected call number five, modeled after Didi's personal whistle. I'd repeat that particular call, hoping the dolphins would begin to associate it with me. We were all clear that we were not attempting to set up a communication based on this symbol. What we were trying to communicate was the *fact* that we were trying to communicate. While I played the repertoire of calls, Steve would record both the output of the synthesizer and the dolphins' vocal reactions. The frequency reducer in the recorder would enable him to hear far more of the dolphins' vocalizations than the rest of us.

At ten thirty in the morning, we arrived at the location where we'd been finding the dolphins regularly and picked up a group of spotters on the bow. After giving them a ten-minute ride, I told Captain Mike to drop anchor. Steve and I went over the side. We were filled with a mixture of anticipation and skepticism as we took the twenty-foot "elevator ride" to the bottom. Howard was behind us with his camera, and Julia just behind him with her slate. Steve held the recorder and stuck the hydrophone, attached to a yard-long piece of fishing pole, into the sand. I knelt on the bottom propping the call generator on my knee.

Several dolphins were in the area, though none seemed particularly interested in the four human figures standing on the sand bottom. I looked over at Steve, his curly black hair floating Medusa-like in the water, as he twisted dials and pushed buttons on his recorder. I pushed the button that set the computer to individual call numbers. The call selected for broadcast was illuminated in large red numerals.

Steve signaled thumbs up. The recorder was working, and he could hear dolphins outside the range of visibility. I inhaled deeply, floating slightly upward as I did, and pressed call number one, a fluttering whistle. Dolphins appeared instantly, sonaring intensely, but swam past. I tried call number two, a descending middle-range tone. Another dolphin, unknown to me, swept by. They were excited but clearly apprehensive. The ungainly visitors to this remote world had finally come up with something different and the dolphins went into investigative mode.

Call number three brought four dolphins over, three adults and a juvenile, but they were too far away to identify. They were in a loose formation, swimming very slowly, barely moving their tail flukes as they circled, inspecting us visually and with their sonar. They were uneasy and soon rose slowly toward the surface and disappeared.

I skipped call number five, wanting to try the others before locking into my own signature call. When I made call number seven, three dolphins poking in the sand twenty yards away swam off immediately. I worried I might have said something to offend them. But how could that be? There was no meaning in any of these calls, as far as we knew, though it's possible the sound itself was somehow unpleasant to them. I quickly switched to call number five, the analog of Didi's signature whistle and repeated it several times. Six dolphins appeared. Then I felt a tap on my shoulder and flinched; it was Steve, who pointed toward the surface.

The author and Steve Gagne transmit and record dolphin sounds

© Howard Hall 1981

Above us, a single dolphin, large and heavily spotted, was sinking tail first. Doing this required him to use his eight-inch-long pectoral fins to maintain a vertical position, not an easy thing for him to do. It was clear that this dolphin was doing something that did not come naturally. His actions involved something that required intention. Performing this action in front of us clearly implied he wanted us to see what he was doing. This dolphin was intending some form of communication to us. It was not a random action. It was a response to our synthesized calls. From its distinctive wide-eyed expression, I recognized the dolphin as Big Eye; turns out he actually does have big eyes. But what was he saying?

Just before reaching the bottom, Big Eye broke this upright posture and swam quickly to the surface for a breath then dove immediately again to the bottom and approached us slowly. I continued to make the number five signature whistle call. Big Eye swam straight toward me, moving very slowly, but turned away at a distance of fifteen feet. He circled again. Steve pulled off his underwater earphones and handed them to me. Listening through the frequency reducer, I could hear that Big Eye was exactly duplicating the calls I was making on the synthesizer. Steve and I looked at each other in amazement.

Big Eye then swam to Howard, who was lying on the sand filming, and slowly allowed himself to sink into a prone position on the sand just six feet away. He lay on the sand in front of Howard for perhaps fifteen seconds, then returned to the surface for a quick breath of air.

Big Eye returned to the bottom and glided toward Steve and me, swimming no more than two feet off the bottom in a horizontal plane. He slowed and dropped his tail to touch the sand; then, anchoring himself to the bottom with his tail flukes and fanning his pectoral fins with great effort, he pulled himself slowly into a vertical position. Steve and I looked at each other, and even through the glass in our facemasks, we could see that we each understood something extraordinary was happening. There could be no doubt that this dolphin was responding to our audio output. But what exactly was he saying? What did this series of gestures mean?

And then it hit me. Howard had been lying prone on the sand and Big Eye had dropped onto the sand in a prone position right in front of him. Steve and I were standing on the bottom looking at one another and that is what Big Eye was now doing. Standing, tail flukes on bottom. Looking at us. For humans, the act of standing is natural. For Big Eye, it required a difficult and purposeful act. And all the while, he was mimicking the sounds I was making with the call generator.

Big Eye was communicating to us in the same way we were communicating to him—through mimicry, physical as well as vocal. My interpretation of the communication was "I perceive you. I know you are there and that you perceive me. I see what you are doing and I am doing the same thing back. I know you are communicating and I am answering you."

Big Eye then flicked his tail fluke and began to ascend, picking up speed as he went. He broke through the surface and executed a series of leaps, then dove quickly to again position himself in front of us, swimming in the normal horizontal posture. Now each time I made my signature whistle, Big Eye duplicated it exactly. Then he began to add two notes of his own to the basic call.

My call was up-down-up. He mimicked the up-down-up, then added two quick tweets. I stopped cold. All I could do was repeat call number five. Again Big Eye tried to elaborate on that call. I could do nothing but switch calls. Big Eye went back to call five "plus," his elaboration of our original, but I could not follow. I was embarrassed that he might think we were nothing more than Johnny-one-notes.

After trying to advance the conversation several more times, Big Eye swam off. Steve and I returned to the surface, stunned by our success and yet frustrated that we could not follow where this brilliant dolphin had tried to lead. The call box was hardwired, preprogrammed, and could not, at least at that time, respond to his inventions.

Julia had already dropped her scuba gear and was snorkeling alone at the surface. Big Eye and two subadults, ages three to six, swam near her, and it was obvious something had changed in the dolphins' attitude toward us. Julia was trying to get sexual identifications and made surface dives to a depth of fifteen feet, rolling on her side to look at the dolphins' underbellies. The dolphins began to coordinate their dives perfectly to hers, diving when she did and returning to the surface with her. There was an attitude of profound gentleness and trust, even respect, in them that had not been there before.

At the surface, the dolphins lined up in front of Julia, perhaps making a statement of hierarchy by their positions. But, though they were leading her, they were exquisitely aware of every move she made. Big Eye and now two subadults were once more mimicking or matching the movements of the human visitors.

Again at the surface, Big Eye positioned himself in front of Julia and slowed. She closed the distance between them from five feet to three, then to two and reached out her hand. Instead of moving away, Big Eye dropped his tail and began twitching in a manner reminiscent of a child who wants to be tickled but flinches every time its parent reaches to do it. Julia's hand came within inches of Big Eye's fluke, but in the end he couldn't allow it, flicked his tail and broke off the contact.

Steve and I were anxious to be back with the dolphins, so we dropped the scuba gear and went into the water with mask, fins, and snorkel, carrying the Plexiglas devices. I made call number five, and for a minute or two, nothing happened. I switched calls to number one, then three, avoiding number seven. Suddenly a phalanx of dolphins came storming into view, swimming very quickly and directly at us, turning only at the last instant. It was the Heavies in perfect formation, absolutely synchronized in their movements and sonaring us intensely. I don't know where they'd been during the previous encounter with Big Eye or whether Big Eye was now among them. Things were happening so quickly that it was impossible to get individual identifications.

I dove to the bottom, operating the call generator and twisting and turning in the clear, warm water. Suddenly Didi arrived with Chopper and Stubby, her behavior characteristically light and inquisitive and very different from the Heavies. She swam to within two feet of my face and looked straight at me. Everyone knew something was happening out there, and it was as exciting for the dolphins as it was for us.

Behind the Heavies came four bottlenose dolphins drawn by the excitement. They appeared huge in comparison with the spotters and less willing to approach us. But they were extremely excited and demonstrated this by trying to mate with the female spotters, and in some cases, they were successful. This was the closest we'd ever been to bottlenose dolphins in the water.

By now it was late afternoon, and the scene had turned into a melee of humans and dolphins diving, turning, and vocalizing, we via Plexiglas boxes and the dolphins in their natural manner. A real conversation had begun, handicapped by the need to communicate not across a barrier of language but between two different universes, but real nonetheless. The dolphins seemed to have finally concluded that there was a kind of intelligence in us after all. We were, at least, no longer mute.

We swam in the mid-afternoon light under a lapis-blue Bahamian sky, cumulus clouds building and billowing brilliant white. We swam in fifteen feet of water over an undersea desert that stretched to the limits of visibility. And as we swam, each of us knew something absolutely astonishing and deeply moving had happened.

I had what I'd been after: contact with these marvelous creatures; contact like I used to have with my dogs when we would race through the woods together; contact you can have with teammates during an intensely played game; contact you can have with a lover or a baby; contact that did not depend on intellectual understanding but was utterly real. And it was to be just the beginning. We'd made contact with mind in the waters.

In 1981, devastating inflation hit the United States. Interest rates climbed to a point where money market funds were paying 15 percent. A severe recession followed, and our bookings for 1982 collapsed. When it became clear we couldn't fill a boat as large as *Tropic Bird*, I went back to *Cloudesley*. Our two weeks on the banks that year gave us more identifications, but bad weather frequently interfered with the work.

In the spring of 1983, on a whale watch out of Boston, I ran into Walter Cronkite with whom I'd worked at CBS News until 1971. He asked what I was doing, and when I told him I'd left CBS, he seemed shocked. Maybe he was thinking that people just don't leave CBS News. But he was interested in the tale I had to tell about dolphins and called over Sir Peter Scott, (son of Captain Robert Falcon Scott, known as Scott of the Antarctic for his ill-fated expedition to the South Pole), and one of the world's great ornithologists and painters of birds and tropical fish.

After hearing my story, Peter asked directly if he and his wife could join one of our trips to White Sand Ridge. I invited him on the spot, hoping to get Bob Gascoine to split their fare with me. Bob agreed immediately, apparently loving the idea of getting to spend time with someone so revered in Britain.

Peter was thrilled with the expedition, and Chopper followed him around like a pet dog. "Maybe he's intrigued by an elderly, fat, bald version of the humans he is used to," Sir Peter mused.

Our third day out, we learned of a hurricane moving toward the banks from the southeast. First indications were that it had passed east of us and was now in open water to the north and thus no longer a threat. But as I looked to the north, I could see a massive weather system moving toward us. Swells were building to eight feet. I asked Bob what the NOAA weather report was saying and was stunned when he told me his radio was not operational.

I decided to go in the water with the dolphins to see how they reacted to category 1-hurricane conditions. They loved it, gliding down the waves, circling over to me, and then bolting off to jump from wave top to wave top. I tried surfing the waves, but the breaks were not acute enough to ride. After an hour in the water, I climbed back aboard *Cloudesley*. The skies were darkening, and the swell continued to build. Bob didn't seem concerned, but I sure was. There was a portable radio aboard, and I raised a faint signal out of Palm Beach. The report was alarming. The hurricane had turned back south and was heading straight for us.

Bob sprung to. Everyone was aboard. We pulled anchor and headed south in a following sea on a course that ran in deep water just off the banks. As the afternoon wore on and evening came, the winds intensified. Water was pouring into my cabin from the hatches and seams. I tried to secure all the camera gear against water and the slamming of the ship.

An hour after sunset, I went topside only to learn that the main sail Bob had set to stabilize the ship had blown. One of the volunteers who had a lot of sailing experience suggested that we anchor and ride out the storm facing into the wind.

Bob then informed us that the anchor rope was so frayed that it would surely snap.

Cool. No radio, blown mainsail, and essentially no anchor; nothing to do but continue south toward West End. And that Bob accomplished superbly. He used the trailing waves to move us forward with jib and staysail set. We were surfing more than sailing. I don't think anyone was dwelling on it, but we were in mortal danger. If we foundered, we were goners just as the crew of the *Maravilla* had been.

Well after midnight, we saw the light marking the entrance to West End harbor. Bob announced to all on deck that we had only one chance to get it right. He had to line up the approach, then turn 60 degrees left and let the waves push us through the narrow opening to the harbor. A mistake would put us on the rocks.

Well, he made as pretty a move as one could imagine, turning the boat like a surfer cutting a curl. Moments later the motion in the boat ceased, and we motored into the safety of the harbor and tied up to the dock. Sir Peter called Bob's handling of the ship the most masterful job of seamanship he'd ever seen. Chloe, Bob's cat, who only appears when the boat is at land, ambled over to the gangplank and went ashore. The rest of us went to sleep in very wet sheets.

The following morning dawned bright, clear, and calm, and we headed back to dolphin territory. Our return to the White Sand Ridge produced one of the most magical events I ever experienced with the dolphins.

By now, the huge breakthroughs of the initial years— the identification of large numbers of individuals and social groups and the mimicry communication via the underwater sound system—had given way to incremental discoveries. We stopped playing with the dolphins in favor of spending hours in the water drifting with them as they went about dolphin business. It felt like becoming a member of their school. What we learned was astonishing.

It had long been theorized that toothed whales—from dolphins to orcas to sperm whales—have the ability to use intense bursts of sonar to stun their prey. But it had never been observed directly, much less filmed. One day while snorkeling in twelve feet of water, I saw dolphins gliding over the bottom rotating their heads from side to side in a tight arc while emitting sharp bursts of sonar. Looking more closely I could see they were training these sonic blasts on pearly razorfish, bottom dwellers about two inches long.

When hit by the dolphins' sonar, the small fish would go belly up and a dolphin would casually glide over and eat it. I watched for fifteen or twenty minutes as one dolphin after another snacked. A bonito hung at the periphery of the action, perhaps hoping to grab a bite or maybe just curious.

One of the dolphins swam over and regurgitated a fish in front of me. I took it as a friendly offering of food but just couldn't bring myself to gobble it up. The dolphin waited a moment, then reclaimed the small fish and swallowed it.

The tactic of deemphasizing play in favor of observing was not an absolute. I had brought two windup toys, each about six inches in length, onto the boat. Late one afternoon in golden light, Julia and I got in the water to see how the dolphins would react to something we knew to be inanimate.

The first toy I tried was a windup gorilla. It made a clicking sound and beat its chest. The dolphins showed no interest in it. Next, I pulled out a red windup fish. It made a clicking sound and swung its tail from side to side. Didi came racing in, followed by Chopper. She took the fish on her nose and started blasting it with prey stunning sonar. The little fish kept swimming. Didi blasted harder. The fish flicked its tail until it ran out of spring wind. I swam over, grabbed it, and twisted the crank on the plastic fish's belly. It sprang to life again, bringing Didi and Chopper over to scrutinize what manner of beast this was.

The amazing thing is that they seemed to recognize it as a fish, although plastic, red in color, and utterly not up to the capabilities of any fish in the sea. But the dolphins seemed to enjoy the toy immensely, and Sir Peter gave it a name: "The Red Mickey."

At the end of the encounter, Didi swam to the sandy bottom, retrieved a sea cucumber about seven inches long, and swam over. She dropped what I knew to be one of her favorite delicacies in front of me. I took it and made squeaking sounds to show appreciation. Then she swam off.

The next day, the dolphins were back looking for fun, but we knew we had to provide something new. As the dolphins drifted by me, I took off my T-shirt and let it float in the water. To my delight, Didi came by, picked it up with her beak, and swam off a few yards. Chopper approached her, and Didi passed the T-shirt to him. He let it slip to his pectoral fin and then to his tail and eventually dropped it in front of Julia, who then returned it to me.

We were both amazed. The dolphins seemed to recognize that the T-shirt belonged to us. Equally a marvel was that we had co-created another game with the dolphins.

A wonderful thing came out of the summer of 1983, aside from surviving it. Peter reinforced our belief in the value of our work when he said, "What you have here with these dolphins is an utterly unique and unprecedented opportunity to study intelligent animals in the open ocean on an ongoing basis."

Didi and her friends
playing with the Scarlet
Micky.
August 1983

Sir Peter Scott's drawing of Didi and friends with Red Mickey
A gift from artist to author.

Perhaps the most compelling evidence of how the dolphins felt about us came in 1985 late in the afternoon after a day of filming. Howard Hall, Julia, and other members of the underwater crew had climbed aboard the *Zodiak* that covered us as we worked at any distance from the main boat. I lingered at the surface, enjoying the delirious late afternoon light, my camera hanging in my right hand. The blue skies above held huge, gleaming white cumulous clouds, and toward the western horizon, blazing orange rays of sunlight shone out of the sea. The water temperature was in the high eighties. I lay on my back and experienced bliss.

Half a dozen young spotted dolphins, including a band of juveniles we'd named the Gang of Four, swam slowly over the sandy bottom thirty feet below. Occasionally, one dolphin would bite another on the tail and begin a brief, friendly tussle consisting of darting, twisting, and jaw snapping. But mostly they were grazing for bottom fish.

In the distance, at the limit of visibility, another sleek, gray creature appeared, swimming in an unusual, sine-wave manner and hugging the bottom. Its tail was not stroking up and down; it was slashing from side to side. The tail fin was vertical, and the head broad and flat. This wasn't a dolphin. It was a very large Atlantic hammerhead shark, one of the few shark species that will attack humans. The shark moved toward me, angling first to one side then the other as though following a scent, probably mine. It was swinging its eyeballs, stuck out on the extremities of the head, so as to see its target first with one eye, then the other, perhaps to gauge distance. I didn't feel comfortable presenting the hammerhead with the sight of my dangling legs, so I jackknifed and dove toward the bottom, raising my camera. Not only was this a unique chance to document the behavior of dolphins around sharks but raising the camera also served to put some metal between the fast-approaching predator and me.

The shark was grayish brown and about eleven feet long. I could judge its size easily because it was twice the length of the subadult dolphins swimming nearby. It undulated across the bottom, its movements now excited and menacing. I'd been diving with hammerheads in the Pacific on numerous occasions and had never felt threatened, but Atlantic hammerheads have a nasty reputation, and this one displayed the agonistic postures that precede an attack.

I hung in the water five feet over the bottom, and sooner than usual, my lungs began to ache for air. In a moment, I'd have to return to the surface. The shark turned directly toward me and accelerated with a flick of its tail. It happened so quickly that I could only react by pulling my camera tight against my body, poised to thrust it against the shark's sensitive rostrum if it struck at me. I turned the camera on.

Suddenly the undersea world came alive with high-pitched whistles and intense sonar bursts. Two juvenile dolphins, Chopper and Stubby, appeared over my left shoulder. I flinched as I felt the wash they created streaking through the water straight for the hammerhead. In an instant, two buddies joined them, bolting in from the right.

The Gang of Four worked as a unit, diving and turning in unison like a squadron of fighter planes flying precision maneuvers.

The hammerhead saw the onrushing dolphins and, looking harassed and perplexed, jerked to the side, away from me. With powerful beats of their tail flukes, the dolphins launched themselves toward the shark's head, clicking and whistling intensely, turning away only at the last instant. Again and again the juvenile dolphins dived at the hammerhead, mobbing it the way sparrows do a hawk, using sonar bursts to attack the shark's lateral lines, a highly sensitive component of the shark sensory system, disorienting the huge fish.

The shark now wanted nothing more than to escape from this sudden torment. It turned one way then another but the Gang of Four were allowing it to move only in one direction—away from me. The hammerhead disappeared into the blue-green distance, and the dolphins, now tremendously excited, swam for the surface to do a series of victory leaps. One after another, they launched themselves through the surface, reentering instants later. After perhaps half a dozen leaps, Chopper cruised up to me, whistling intensely. I swam with him at the surface, trying my best to move in a way that showed the same kind of exuberance he'd displayed, but my human body dragged in the water and he had to restrain himself to stay with me. He was too excited to maintain the slow pace and darted off with his friends.

I was frankly glad to have footage of the dolphins saving me from the hammerhead. Without it, there might have been quite a bit of skepticism about this event. Some people just don't want to admit animals are capable of altruism. Of course, the incident made a fabulous scene in the film we would eventually title *In the Kingdom of the Dolphins.*

PBS picked up the film to play during the pledge period in December 1985. Looking at the film on air, rather than in a cutting room, gave me a different perspective on what we had accomplished. Over the years since our first encounter, we had continued to be excited at each encounter with the dolphins and the sense of awe never diminished.

As I watched the film in its entirety, knowing millions of others were also tuned in, the magnitude of what we'd accomplished sank in. We'd spent hundreds of hours over the course of seven years in a remote area of the Bahamas with a pod of wild dolphins. We had created relationships and maybe even friendships. Our two species had collaborated in creating a rudimentary but nonetheless profound communication in the form of mimicry.

Actually what we created might more aptly be called meta-communication. We communicated that we wanted to communicate and that we each recognized the other species had the ability to communicate. The acts of playing, exchanging toys, even just being in close proximity were communications of trust and affinity.

But the capper was the fact that four young dolphins had saved me from attack by a hammerhead shark. The footage proves what happened. And what other conclusion can one come to but that the dolphins were willing to risk their lives to save mine. If you take even a moment to think about it, you cannot avoid the conclusion that this relationship with the dolphins has profound implications for how we treat dolphins, whales and other animal life forms.

After 1985, we did not go to the Bahamas every summer. PBS hired Julia and me to make a film in Africa and India, then Audubon commissioned a film on whales and in 1988, A&E commissioned a twenty-six-part series we called *Challenge of the Seas*, narrated by Ted Danson. In succeeding years, we would find what we had considered a unique relationship with the spotted dolphins in the Bahamas was actually available with other species of dolphin, with sperm whales, and even with killer whales in places as diverse as Rangiroa Atoll in French Polynesia, Tysfjord in arctic Norway, the Galapagos Islands and the West Indies.

But I did not abandon the *Maravilla* dolphins. I've been back many times and done a lot more film work. Many of our greatest discoveries were still ahead.

~ 5 ~

Lethal Waters

During 1986 and 1987, I was shooting a film on whales for the National Audubon Television series airing on Turner Broadcasting. The project took me to the Portuguese island of Madeira off Morocco, Cape Cod, the West Indies, and the Galapagos. In the Galapagos, off Isabella Island, I had my first chance to film a sperm whale in the water. These massive creatures behaved very much like the dolphins in the Bahamas, approaching me for a look and moving their bodies and flukes to avoid injuring me.

We had just finished editing the film when, in the summer of 1987, an alarming series of reports came across the newswires and television reporting that an unusual number of bottlenose dolphins were washing ashore dead along the coast of New Jersey.

A *New York Times* article headed "Search Widening for Clues in Puzzle of Mounting Dolphin Deaths" reported that some one hundred dolphins had been found dead along the shores of New Jersey and the die-off was moving farther south. An increasing number of dolphins were being found stranded in Virginia, all of them with bronchial pneumonia, and virtually all of them dead. The article noted that hundreds of dolphins had almost certainly died in deep water and would never be counted. There was real panic along the Jersey shore. In the absence of reliable information, hypotheses blossomed among the citizens of beach towns. Was this a form of dolphin AIDS? Had deadly toxins escaped from a military facility nearby?

My film on whales was followed by a contract to do a one-hour special on dolphins, again for Audubon on Turner Broadcasting. I was to cover the wonders of dolphins in the wild but executive producer Chris Palmer told me in no uncertain terms that there was also a strong mandate from Ted Turner to hit conservation issues hard. The film, which was eventually titled *If Dolphins Could Talk*, gave me a chance to investigate the die-off. I flew to New Jersey.

As I began to look into this unfolding tragedy, I remembered visiting Atlantic City, a glorious stretch of beach, as a very young boy. The memory still evoked the smell of Coppertone and salt air. At that time and through the early encounters with the dolphins in the Bahamas the ocean remained a place of joy and innocence. Now, it appeared paradise might be slipping away.

The National Marine Fisheries Service (NMFS) calls such die-offs "unusual mortality events," or UMEs. This UME had first been detected by Bob Schoelkopf of the Brigantine Marine Mammal Stranding Network as early as April. Dolphins were washing ashore and beachgoers reported their eyes were stinging. Some even reported nausea. No one knew whether there was a connection to the dolphin deaths.

As May turned into June, the numbers of dead dolphins washing up on beaches had increased to the point that Schoelkopf called federal authorities. It was the beginning of a medical mystery with ramifications of the highest importance for dolphins and humans alike. While dolphins and small whales strand for a variety of reasons, nothing of this magnitude had ever been reported. The event was telling us something about the health of the oceans, and it was crucial we find out what the message was.

When it became clear that the dead dolphins on beaches were not isolated events, an interagency governmental task force was formed. Representatives from agencies such as the NMFS and state and local health departments swarmed the beaches looking for evidence.

Dr. Joseph Geraci, the man chosen to head the task force, known as the dolphin response team, was a well-known and highly respected marine pathologist from the University of Guelph in Ontario, Canada. As the UME progressed, Dr. Geraci came under tremendous pressure to find what was killing the dolphins.

But few of the dead dolphins could be necropsied due to decomposition. Where necropsy was possible high levels of contaminants such as polychlorinated biphenyls (PCBs) were found. So every cadaver recovered had to be treated as toxic waste and disposed of by a HazMat team. By August, dolphins were stranding on Virginia beaches and the total number of confirmed dead had reached six hundred.

When I interviewed Bob Schoelkopf at the Marine Mammal Stranding Center, he told me, "We may be losing the entire near-shore population of bottlenose dolphins along our Atlantic Coast." He listed their symptoms. All the dolphins had fluid in their chests, stomachs, and lungs. Most were emaciated, indicating that they hadn't eaten in days, or even weeks. In addition, their mouths were lacerated, and on some, their skin was peeling. "All their internal organs were pathologic, with enlarged spleens and other abnormalities," he said. Tissue samples from the Virginia dolphins were sent to the National Veterinary Service Laboratories in Ames, Iowa, one of the country's leading facilities for studying animal pathology. As summer dissolved into fall and the die-off spread southward, no diagnosis was forthcoming.

To me, the die-off was an utterly horrifying experience. I imagined individual dolphins like Didi and Chopper first feeling that something was wrong, then growing sicker and more vulnerable to shark attack and finally dying in agony. And as stranded dolphins were found on beaches of the southeastern United States, I was haunted by the idea that the lethal agent might leap the Gulf Stream and infect the spotted dolphins I knew and loved in the Bahamas.

After completion of *If Dolphins Could Talk*, I continued my investigation of the UME, financed by a grant from the Center for Marine Conservation. During that inquiry, some very peculiar things happened.

I flew from California to New Jersey and drove along the eastern seaboard. During the fall of 1987, a top vet from the National Veterinary Service (NVS) pulled me aside at one of the many public meetings held in coastal communities to try to allay the fears of coastal dwelling humans. "I will only speak to you on the absolute condition that you do not associate my name with what I'm about to tell you," he began.

I agreed but wondered why all the secrecy.

"What's going on involves the fact that these dolphins are loaded with chemicals such as PCBs, pesticides, and other contaminants. The way these chemicals work is that they bioaccumulate up the marine food chain, and because they're lipophilic [easily absorbable by fat] they can build to very high levels in dolphins, whales, and other marine mammals."

The absolute levels of contamination in the water column are very low and safe, he went on to tell me. "The chemical companies that dump these contaminants think that by diluting the poisons they render them effectively harmless." What they didn't count on was the reverse process taking place as these chemicals are biomagnified up the food chain. The chemicals are absorbed by plankton that are eaten by tiny fish, which are then eaten by small fish, then larger fish, and ultimately by dolphins and humans. "By the time they reach apex predators—including us—they're literally concentrated by factors of billions," he said, his face contorted by the thought. The chemical companies' theory of "dilution is the solution" did not contemplate the unfathomable ways of nature.

The sad tale went on. Dolphins can survive for a long time with very high levels of contamination because the toxic material is bound in the blubber. But if the food supply is limited and a dolphin doesn't get enough to eat, it will mobilize its fat reserves to compensate, and the toxins will flood into the blood stream and tissues. The dolphins found on the beaches were certainly emaciated.

"I will tell you this and I'm not exaggerating," my source continued. "Dolphins and whales worldwide are in danger of extirpation—complete annihilation—from these chemicals. These persistent organic pollutants and heavy metals break down immune systems and act as estrogen imitators. They feminize males and superfeminize females. That will disrupt reproduction in any of the mammals that have large amounts of blubber in which the chemicals accumulate."

It was a staggering assessment. I asked him why he wanted me to maintain such secrecy, expecting him to tell me he was bound by some confidentiality agreement or government restriction. It was far more banal than that.

"I'll be retiring in less than two years, and I can't afford to put my pension in jeopardy by stirring up controversy."

I was speechless. Say what? He wouldn't reveal a threat to every dolphin on earth, not to mention humans, so as not to endanger his pension? He walked away without another word. I hope he's enjoying his retirement.

While the dire prediction the gentleman from NVS had made served to alert me to the extreme crisis dolphins faced worldwide, I couldn't disseminate it. Without a source who would own statements so profoundly alarming, I was hamstrung. I couldn't put them in my film. I'd need an on-camera interview for that, and he certainly wasn't about to go on camera. No respectable print outlet would publish such information from an anonymous source. But I was forewarned about the depth of the threat facing dolphins and that spurred my search for answers that went far beyond a single UME.

In March 1988, the last bottlenose dolphin associated with the die-off was found at Cape Canaveral in east central Florida.

For nearly a decade, I'd been trying to stop the slaughter of dolphins by tuna seiners and Japanese fishermen. The Atlantic Coast die-off represented something far more pervasive and lethal than even the worst atrocities I'd dealt with and brought me a sense of dread and despair.

In May 1989, the oversight subcommittee of the House Merchant Marine and Fisheries committee held hearings on the die-off. Beginning in the early summer of 1987, congressional representatives from states along the eastern seaboard had been hearing from constituents about burning eyes and loss of tourist revenue as vacationers avoided fun-in-the-sun locations such as Cape May, New Jersey, and Virginia Beach. Dead dolphins littering the shoreline had opened questions that were deeply alarming. There wasn't yet a mob carrying torches, but people wanted answers.

I flew to Washington, D.C., hired a camera crew, and set up in the ornate House hearing room where experts on marine mammals and ocean toxics were gathering.

As part of compiling data for my report on the die-off I had gone to Washington to interview authorities at NOAA, NMFS and the Smithsonian Institution. One of my interviewees informed me that Dr. Geraci, the head of the response team, was trying to get in touch with me and gave me a callback number. Geraci had avoided answering my questions on several previous occasions, so now I thought, "Great. Maybe he has some important information for me."

I phoned the number that had been left for me and when he answered I said, "Hello, Dr. Geraci; this is Hardy Jones. I understand you've been trying to reach me."

His accusatory reply stunned me. "I'm told you've been running all over Washington asking all sorts of questions. What do you think you're doing?"

I resisted the impulse to tell him to bugger himself, took a breath, and said, "I really don't understand your question or your tone. I have every right as an American citizen and a journalist to question officials of my government. What's your issue with this?"

Geraci seemed to realize he wasn't going to get very far with an intimidating approach and settled down. "Well, I'm just interested in all aspects of this situation." We rang off after a modicum of civility had been restored.

How can one evaluate his extreme agitation at my inquiries? Is it simply that he was under tremendous pressure and so behaved brusquely and inappropriately? Or was there fear somewhere that I might discover something that someone didn't want discovered?

The interagency team issued a preliminary report in 1988 that some eight hundred dolphins had died and washed ashore but that thousands more might have died at sea and not been counted. The report estimated that 50 percent or more of the coastal migratory stock of bottlenose dolphins between Florida and New Jersey had died during this period and ended with chilling words. "The overwhelming nature of some of the infections, which probably arose in the lung, may have been related to immunoincompetence, the cause of which cannot be established."

But the official findings would be delivered by Dr. Geraci to the House subcommittee. He postulated that the trigger that led to the UME was the dolphins eating fish that had accumulated brevetoxin, the toxic byproduct of what is commonly called red tide. Red tide is a naturally occurring phenomenon but one that has been increasing worldwide both in incidence and intensity. He based this conclusion on the results of necropsies of only seventeen dolphins of the hundreds that had died. Within that small sample, only seven dolphins had displayed traces of brevetoxin in their systems. His conclusion satisfied virtually no one.

Other scientists testifying before the committee, as well as members of Congress, were scathing in their remarks. Representative Frank Pallone of New Jersey, where the die-off first evidenced itself, said, "It is just as likely that toxic chemicals such as PCBs or other chemical contaminants are the cause of this tragic event."

Congresswoman Claudine Schneider of Rhode Island reported that one of the dolphins necropsied had "6,800 parts per million of PCBs in its blubber." That is a huge level of intoxication.

Equally shocking was the testimony of Dr. William Evans, Undersecretary for Oceans and Atmosphere, who testified, that "in my experience almost every dolphin we've found has high levels of chlorinated hydrocarbons." Chlorinated hydrocarbons are often referred to as POPs, persistent organic pollutants. PCBs are a form of POP. Given that such chemicals are known immunosuppressors, I personally found Geraci's conclusion weak at best.

What led Geraci to placing the prime responsibility for the UME on brevetoxin is open to speculation. The evidence he cited was minimal. But he had been under intense pressure to produce an answer. The fact that he blamed a naturally occurring phenomenon rather than man-made chemicals for the catastrophe raised questions that linger to this day.

Dr. Pierre Beland, a French Canadian now with the St. Lawrence National Institute of Ecotoxicology, concluded his testimony before the committee by saying, "We still do not know what happened along the eastern seaboard of the United States in 1987." It would take many more years before a satisfactory explanation was presented.

The process of reviewing evidence and getting it peer-reviewed takes time. In September 1994, I received a report of the conclusions of the interagency team that had gathered in Beaufort, North Carolina, with additional experts to bring together all information produced by investigations into the die-off. The report concluded, "The results for the beach-cast specimens (dead dolphins) obviously reflect the levels of contaminants in the nearshore environment where the dolphins accumulate these substances." The study clearly placed blame on man-made pollutants.

A second major UME involving morbillivirus killed several thousand striped dolphins along the Spanish Mediterranean coast from 1990 to 1992, followed by another in 2007. And significant die-offs of bottlenose dolphins have occurred along the coasts of Texas and Florida in the Gulf of Mexico, though nothing of the magnitude of the 1987 – 1988 UME along the east coast. Another catastrophic die-off occurred in the North Sea during the late 1980s, killing some twenty thousand seals, perhaps half of all Europe's population of these animals.

In 1991, Turner Broadcasting released *If Dolphins Could Talk*. It was brilliantly narrated by Michael Douglas. The final words of the script dealing with the die-off were, "The level of PCBs in the oceans is increasing and could reach levels that threaten the extinction of marine mammals." Since then the situation has gotten worse rather than better.

If Dolphins Could Talk represented a break with the films I had done to date. My strategy of affecting policy change with images of their beauty and intelligence just didn't seem to work. I would now embark on a series of high-impact films that directly addressed the tragedies facing dolphins and other marine mammals. I especially had in mind ending the massacre of dolphins in the Eastern Tropical Pacific (ETP) tuna fishery.

For reasons unknown, dolphins and tuna associate in the ETP. When purse-seine netting replaced hook-and-line fishing, the fishermen on the tuna boats would find their intended prey by finding dolphins. They would run the dolphins to exhaustion and then set a net around them. The tuna would be trapped in the same net under the dolphins. It is estimated that a total of more than six million dolphins had died entangled in the nets over the years.

If Dolphins Could Talk contained footage by a young environmentalist named Sam LaBuddie. Sam had boarded a Panamanian tuna clipper as a cook. He carried a small video camera and ran around the ship manically videotaping everything that happened. He had set himself up so that when dolphins were wrapped in a tuna net off the coast of Costa Rica, his presence with a camera would not stir suspicion. The footage Sam brought back, at great risk to his life, showed grotesque scenes of dolphins dying in the nets and on the decks of the tuna vessels.

I licensed the footage for use in the TBS/Audubon film. When the show hit the air, the results were explosive. The emotional impact of the footage was amplified by a short PSA hosted by George C. Scott that included a 900 number, produced for the show by Stan Minasian of the Marine Mammal Fund. The result was a pile of six thousand telegrams hitting the desk of the chairman of Starkist tuna demanding an end to catching tuna by setting nets on dolphins.

Within weeks, Starkist announced that it would no longer accept tuna caught on dolphin. The dolphin-safe label was born and is today overseen by Earth Island Institute and the Marine Mammal Fund. My film synergized with years of hard work by several organizations and was a major conservation victory.

What again became clear to me was that film or video of horrific events such as the dolphin slaughters in Japan or the drowning of hundreds of thousands of dolphins in the tuna fishery, could produce a huge public response. But my outreach still depended on getting television contracts for documentaries that required eighteen months to produce. They had their impact, but there was no follow-up. That all changed with the Internet.

In the late 1980s, I got to know film and television actor Ted Danson during production of *Challenge of the Seas*. Ted and I have remained friends and comrades in arms fighting for the oceans. I joined the board of American Oceans Campaign, which he had founded. In 2000, I showed him how the Internet, even in its nascent state, could expand the impact of our work. He was excited and signed on immediately. Our initial goal was to get a streaming video Web site up and running.

This gave me the ability to go on location with small video cameras and laptops and literally broadcast from the scene of dolphin killings and other environmental crises. We could skip over program commissioners and avoid long lapses in time to bring information to millions around the world almost instantaneously. That enabled concerned citizens to respond to the event immediately through e-mail, online donations and other means.

We called our new non-profit organization BlueVoice.org.

~ 6 ~

Friends in Many Oceans

By the late 1980s, nearly ten years after my first encounter with dolphins, my life's course was being charted by filmmaking assignments as well as my own passions: interacting with dolphins in the open sea and working to end the growing threats to them. When I was lucky, the two coincided. In the beginning, I had thought the spotted dolphins in the Bahamas to be uniquely accessible. But over the years, I found that I could form "eyeball-to-eyeball" relationships with orcas and even sperm whales. My fascination with the spotted dolphins broadened to include other cetaceans in other oceans. Each would reveal some extraordinary aspect of behavior.

By the mid-1980s, the save-the-whale and-dolphin movements had gained traction. In 1986, the International Whaling Commission (IWC) voted for and passed a ten-year moratorium on all whaling. This was a great victory for forces working to protect whales because not only was commercial whaling banned for a decade but a whale sanctuary was also established over the entire Indian Ocean. That same year, the Soviet Union withdrew from whaling, eliminating one of the two nations that had sent factory ships onto the seas of the world to slaughter whales.

Unfortunately, there are loopholes in the IWC charter and immediately upon implementation of the moratorium, Japan, Norway and Iceland began to exploit them. So the urgency to protect whales remained. As mentioned, Chris Palmer, head of Audubon Television, had commissioned a film on whales with an emphasis on conservation issues.

One of the singular moments during the making of the film that would come to be titled simply *Whales!* took place off the coast of Nova Scotia. I'd gone there to film right whales, one of the most endangered species on earth. We found them off Brown's Banks, and I was able to get the first pictures ever of right whales mating underwater.

Right whales are vigorous in courtship. Usually three whales are involved in the process: two males and the intended female. Such a trio appeared off the starboard side of our 110-foot sailboat. Camera in hand, I descended a ladder on the side of the ship. Everyone on board was screaming, "Get in. They're right there. Go! Go!" As though I couldn't see three huge whales only twenty feet away!

Somewhat daunted by the massive size of the whales and the vigor of their movements, I hesitated, then let go of the ladder and dropped into the water. I could see the whales at the surface but not through the plankton-rich water. The boat and whales seemed to converge. I was pushed into the midst of the mating group. My thumb triggered the camera. The whales were barely visible underwater, black Zeppelin-like figures against a dark green background. Then a pink penis, perhaps six feet in length, extended from the belly of one whale and swung directly at my head. I ducked. It was clear it would be suicidal to stay in the water. I could be crushed between the whales and the boat. As I climbed the ladder to the deck, I wondered if it would be ignominious or heroic to have been decapitated by a giant whale penis.

Scott Krauss of the New England Aquarium Right Whale research team leaned over the top of the ladder. "What did you see?"

"They were definitely mating," I shouted back.

"Oh, they don't mate up here," Scott yelled back.

I had the film to prove otherwise, so felt confident when I said, "Well there were ten toes up and ten toes down."

Scott was surprised. Another scientific belief demolished by observing in the water instead of from a boat deck. Once processed and presented in *Whales!* these images undid some long-held scientific opinion that right whales engaged only in courtship displays off the Canadian coast but did not mate there.

The heart of our film was to be a segment on sperm whales in the Galapagos. For me, the chance to be with sperms in their natural environment was a logical extension of our work with the dolphins because they use sound much the way dolphins do. But two other factors made this a tremendously exciting prospect. Sperm whales have the largest brains on earth, and they're the largest of the toothed whales.

The tactic we had in mind was to approach them as though they were simply huge dolphins. This was not a bad plan but given that a sperm whale can easily reach forty-five feet in length and that they spend much of their time hundreds and even thousands of feet underwater, it somewhat underestimated the experience to come.

We spent six days looking for whales, putting in at night at places like Sombrero Chino where the penguins hopped onto rocks beside us, utterly unafraid. The Galapagos was paradise; the animals, innocent. The sun hit a clear horizon, something that hadn't been visible in the Northern Hemisphere for thirty years due to air pollution. Days were brutally hot, and I frequently fell into a stupor, yanking myself awake to keep vigil.

We first found whales about ten miles west of Isla Isabella along the hundred-fathom line. We brought our pathetically small ten-foot inflatable broadside to a traveling quartet of whales. There was a female with a small calf by her side. A second, middle-sized whale pushed the massive bulb of her forehead through a swell and vented into the breeze. She was followed by what looked to be the sperm whale equivalent of a third grader, an animal too young to really want to be on its own but too old to swim contentedly on its mother's flank. They were aware of our presence and perhaps sensed our benevolent intention or harmlessness.

The memory storage and communication sectors of a sperm whale's brain are the largest of any animal on earth. I had no doubt these animals would have heard stories passed from generation to generation—accounts of the days when small boats approaching meant cold steel piercing their fine gray skin, penetrating vital organs and bringing an agonizing death for family and friends.

The whales moved relentlessly but slowly forward and did not dive. That told me they were not panicked by our presence. I slipped over the side of the rubber gunwale and put my head in the water. There was a faint train of *click-click-click*s at intervals of roughly one a second, very different from the buzzing click trains of dolphins. I tried to imitate the click sound but the effort was pathetic, so I tried a sound that would project through the water—anything to raise their curiosity.

Suppressing embarrassment, and it was about what the whales would think, not the people on the boat, I began a long series of whoops and howls into my snorkel. It was the best imitation of a humpback I could muster on short notice, not to mention short breath. Lying on the surface with my head in the water, looking into the distance, I could see nothing but fifty feet of cloudy green water. When I focused close, the sea became a bouillabaisse of tiny translucent critters reflecting sunlight.

Pulling myself upright and timing a series of hard fin strokes with the rise of the swell, I could raise myself out of the water and see the whales blowing like steam engines. They seemed to have stopped moving. I turned to Julia in the boat to get her read on the situation. She yelled down to me, "They've stopped dead in the water. Do that noise again."

I stuck my head back in the water and whooped as loud as I could manage. The sound would be garbled from time to time by water entering my snorkel, but it was loud and would travel in the water. Julia yelled again, "They've stopped. They've definitely stopped, and they're turning toward us."

A thousand miles out in the Pacific, my whooped gibberish had been heard, and my calls had registered in the mind of a sperm whale. And now the whale was focusing on me. The volume of the clicks intensified. As the waves lifted me, I kicked and strained to see over the crests. Julia was pointing and yelling at me. "They're moving. They're coming right at us."

The whales were curious. By God! They were curious. And they were coming straight toward me, looking like a phalanx of locomotives getting up steam. I put my head underwater and stared out through my facemask.

There was a change of color in the bright green surface water of the sea; then, individual shapes formed, moving slowly, effortlessly, relentlessly toward me: a female with a calf on her left side, another female just behind them. The largest female approached so as to pass me on her left. Her course brought her so close that the juvenile was forced to split off from her to avoid running straight into me.

As the female moved to within a few feet, barely beyond the reach of my arm, a sense of tremendous calm descended upon me, not a numb feeling but one of being hyperconscious and intensely alive. This lady whale looked at me with an eye as large as a grapefruit. Her eyeball rotated in its socket to focus on me as she moved past. Relaxed, thrilled, in contact with this other mind, I was riveted to her. In the kind of time measured by a watch, our first meeting happened over half a minute. But in the moment, it was timeless. The experience began in my imagination and extended forever in my memory. I began to be aware of her huge fluke scything toward me, and started to scuttle sideways in the water. But there was no need. She considerately bent her tail to the side, allowing the fluke to pass me by safely. She continued past me, threw her huge flukes into the air to disappear into the plankton layer beneath the thermocline. The experience of being with these whales was like falling in love.

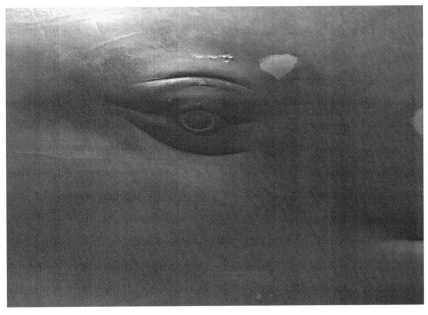

Author's view of sperm whale eye during close encounter

This would not be my only friendly encounter with sperm whales. While advising a French film crew, I used my version of a humpback call to intrigue a male sperm whale off the island of Dominica in the West Indies. The whale was approaching me with a companion. The two began a dive, but when I whooped the larger of the two arched its back and rose to the surface. We swam together eye-to-eye for nearly an hour, all captured by the French video team, in warm, clear Caribbean waters.

The following day, the cameraman and I spent nearly an hour within twenty yards of a female sperm whale, two juveniles, and a newborn. One of the juveniles repeatedly picked up the newborn in her jaws and lifted it to the surface, an indescribably tender and intimate moment.

While these encounters are thrilling, they do not involve thrill seeking; rather, they are attempts to see how far I can go in establishing relationships with fellow large-brained mammals. And they open something in me that is beyond cerebral.

In the early 1980s, I had learned there was someone conducting the same kind of long-term field studies we were doing with spotted dolphins, but he was working with orcas. His name is Ken Balcomb, a research biologist based out of Friday Harbor in the San Juan Islands off Washington State.

Although they're most often referred to as killer whales in English, they're actually the largest species of dolphin and are more properly called orca. The Latin *Orcinus orca* means creature from the underworld. The term killer whale is an intimidating name and I've sometimes wondered if they might not call us "hairless killer apes." Orcas, second largest of the toothed whales, have brains four times larger than human brains and are every bit as complex. They're highly social, living in families presided over by a matriarch. The enormous and powerful males never leave their mothers over their entire lifetimes, which may span fifty to eighty years, and often do not survive her death.

Pods are made up of adult males and females and youngsters who travel together consistently over many years. These pods may break into subpods for short periods, sometimes motivated by the need to find food. But they always regroup. When orcas who have been separated from their main pod for a time reunite, there's tremendous rejoicing, evident in their celebratory play at the surface, which can best be measured by dropping a hydrophone into the water to listen to their symphony of cries and whistles.

As late as the 1960s, U.S. Navy handbooks described orcas as bloodthirsty killers who would attack human beings on sight. Naval aircraft actually used orcas for target practice. That's a hideous thought but a measure of how far we've come in our perception of these creatures in only a few decades.

Ken is a burly, bearded, highly intelligent researcher. He smiles a lot. On my first trip with Ken, I was stunned and inspired by the power of the orcas. Here were creatures forty times heavier than spotted dolphins, moving at eight knots for hours on end. They allowed us so close to them that we were misted with their exhalations.

Just as we'd done, Ken began his study with the daunting task of identifying each whale—the only way to figure out the social structure of the group. He collected an extensive photographic record cataloguing the black-and-white pattern of their saddles and the marks on their dorsal fins.

Slowly, a fascinating picture of orca society began to develop. Three pods frequent these waters. J, K, and L pods are collectively called the southern residents. Each uses slightly different calls indicating there is a dialectical difference among the pods. But that does not prevent them from gathering in superpods, where they socialize and hunt together.

One can hardly imagine the emotional pain these creatures suffer when separated from their families by force. But when orcas became star attractions in marine parks all over the world, they also became the target of a brutal captivity industry.

In the 1960s and 1970s, J, K, and L pods were raided. The captivity team used explosives to drive them into a bay where the young and pretty whales were separated, then hauled away. The depleted pods, missing their young and many females, were then released. By the time Ken began his studies, 58 orcas had been taken from a population of perhaps 120. Citizens of the area who knew the orcas were horrified. Protest grew until in 1973, the state of Washington banned all further captures in state waters. Now these orcas, known individually by name, were protected by law. They seemed to have a fighting chance for recovery.

In 1995, we were commissioned to do a series of six programs about marine mammal babies for Discovery Channel titled *First Breath.* An episode on baby orcas brought us back to the San Juans on several occasions from 1995 through 1996. I spent joyous days on the water with Ken and his son Kelley shooting topside and waterline footage from the boat.

It's illegal to enter the water with orcas or any other marine mammal in U.S. waters. But when doing preproduction for the *First Breath* series I learned of pods of friendly orcas in the Norwegian Arctic. There's no restriction on diving with orcas in Norway so this presented a unique opportunity to film them underwater. As I thought of the impending encounters, I reminded myself that there was no recorded case of an orca harming a human in the wild.

Orcas were abundant in Tysfjord until the early 1980s, when overfishing destroyed the herring stock on which they feed. As the herring population crashed, fishermen started to blame the orcas for taking too many fish and began shooting and harpooning them. They killed as many as eight hundred. The orcas found safety in Iceland where they went to find food and didn't come back to the Tysfjord area until the early 1990s. When they returned, something highly unexpected occurred. The whales that had been brutalized by the fishermen of Arctic Norway were showing curiosity toward divers.

During the intervening eight years, the world had discovered the wonder of whales, and a small whale watching operation opened in Tysfjord, giving commercial value to orcas by bringing tourists to hotels, restaurants, and boat owners. This split the community into pro-whale factions composed of those who now lived off the tourist trade and anti-whale factions who were fishermen afraid the whales would eat their fish.

A few dive-with-orca operations had grown up, attracting people from all over the world to Tysfjord for a chance to swim with the largest of the dolphins.

In 1994, Julia and I had undergone what may be the friendliest separation on record. In part, it was due to working together 24/7 and perhaps to a fourteen-year disparity in our ages. But we continued to make films and in 1995 traveled to Norway to film the orca segment of First Breath.

My first sight of Tysfjord's orca-filled waters embraced by mountains covered in snow, was awe-inspiring. The seas were pewter gray. The sun, covered by deep clouds, here fluffy white, there almost black, front lit the waters and mountains of the fjord producing a magical saturation of light.

Though we think of the Arctic as being universally frigid, eddies from the Gulf Stream warm the western coast of Norway and keep temperatures from plummeting. During most of our days at Tysfjord, the mercury didn't fall below freezing. The gear that has been developed—exposure suits for topside work, dry suits for diving in very cold water, woolly socks, and expedition long johns—enabled me to film for long hours on the boat and enter the water without discomfort. The dry suits work so well there is no sense of shock jumping into nearly freezing water, except to the face, which is the only part of the body exposed.

At six feet six inches tall, Dag Vongraven, the operator of our twenty-six-foot day cruiser, stood eye-to-eye with me. He's a scientist who'd been studying orcas in these waters for ten years. He wore a strange exposure suit: standard orange but with the crotch ripped out. I wondered if he had a need to be able to pee on short notice, but he told me that a seal he was studying had taken a bite out of this area at the juncture of his legs, just missing vital areas of his body.

Deep within the fjords, the world was quiet. Vast ramparts of granite rose on both sides constraining the sea into something like a broad river running through a huge canyon. Several times, members of the pod swam just under our keel and we could see their shapes fifteen feet beneath us.

Filming topside was wondrous. Orcas rose to breathe on a glassy sea that reflected the snow crowned mountains. Each rising of the whales was an event, never less impressive than the times before. The concussions of their exhalations, which started as quicksilver streamers of bubbles underwater, were like gunshots, followed by the subtler whoosh of their inhalation.

Within a couple days, we had some beautiful topside footage, but the real payoff came underwater. I stripped off my exposure suit in which I'd been overly warm and began the excruciating process of preparing to dive. There's no easy or quick way to get into a dry suit and I felt the sweat on my back and neck beginning to freeze.

Once resuited, I swung my legs over the transom and eased myself down onto the swim platform ready to drop into the water. The orcas were playing about one hundred yards away, exhibiting an extraordinary display of energy and power. We came parallel to members of what the scientists who study them call P pod. The whales seemed to get excited. Some of the youngsters porpoised toward the boat. I swallowed and hesitated. There have been no reports of orcas in the wild attacking humans, but in reality, very few humans have been in the water with them. It was my best guess and fondest hope that they wouldn't attack me.

Again, I had a peanut gallery yelling instructions. Dag and Julia and the rest of the crew screamed "Go! Go! Now!" like I was some kind of cowardly cretin for hesitating to leap in front of the onrushing whales. But when I caught sight of one of the calves leaping forward, dolphin-like, my own excitement took over. I slipped off the swim step into the frigid water and spun to locate the orcas. Four members of the pod appeared, moving quickly in the green-black depths, twenty feet below and thirty horizontal feet away. I turned on the camera to get my first ever underwater orca footage but got only one quick pass.

With adrenaline roaring through my veins, I clambered back onto the swim step, stoked beyond the ability to speak. Gasping for air, I pointed toward the orca pod moving rapidly away from us. Dag ran the boat forward until he had us back in their path. My second drop worked better. Three orcas approached and lined up fifteen feet below me. They were young animals, so they appeared to be black-and-white dolphins, only larger, much larger. I was enraptured to be in their sight as they twisted and turned, sonaring me and looking me over with their eyes to get some clue about the nature of this strange creature bobbing at the surface of their universe.

I had four encounters with the members of P pod that day, and the last was the most intense. The orca were swimming parallel to the course of our boat and one of them began to slap its tail on the surface. "Aha," I thought. "This presents an opportunity".

I was standing on deck in my thermal underwear, steam rushing off me as though I'd just stepped out of Hades. I jumped down onto the swim step, grabbed a swim fin, and slapped the surface. The whale slapped again. I slapped back. The whale slapped twice and I slapped twice, whereupon three of the orcas turned and headed directly toward our boat. There is no question they were responding to the sound of my slapping. Mimicry worked here in the Arctic just as it had with the dolphins in the Bahamas.

The next day, we didn't find them until very late, which in Tysfjord in early November means 2:30 p.m. The sunset was visible through a small hole in the dark gray and black cloud banks, casting a spotlight across the surface of the sea from the west. P pod appeared again, and its members exhibited the same behaviors as the day before. They allowed us to close with them and travel among them. By now we felt that we were recognizing and learning the personalities of individuals as we watched them socialize as a family, resting languorously at the surface and then launching into quick bouts of playful aggression.

When we overtook the pod, the captain put the engine in neutral and gave us the go ahead to enter the water. He called out that he had spotted a female orca known to him from previous years, the friendliest of all the whales in Tysfjord. The medium-sized female approached the boat and took position only a few feet under the swim step, just beneath my dangling fins—so close that I had to enter the water by falling off the side of the swim step so as not to land on her.

And there she was: a free orca in the fjords of Norway only a few feet from me. I began to run film through the K-100. The squeaky sound of the old camera's motor seemed to intrigue her; she wagged and slightly rotated her head as she used her sonar.

We swam together for the next hour, two species so apparently alien united by the common thread of intelligence and curiosity. At times, the young female would position herself vertically fifteen feet below the surface, her nose pointing straight up at me, then swim off a short distance to take a breath, only to return a minute later. I was in a state that could only be called rapture. The tune of an old Kirk Douglas movie *The Vikings* played unbidden but thunderously in my mind. I began to hum it very loud. There's no way to know with certainty whether the singing interested this lady orca, but when I stopped, she would drift off, only to return if I began humming the song again.

Eventually she came within two meters of me, resting just beneath the surface, blowing occasionally. She alternated between facing me head-on and swimming past very slowly and looking with the one eye she could turn on me. What was perhaps more astonishing than anything was that I felt completely at home with this huge animal, knowing that what I was doing at that moment was absolutely what I was meant to do in life. As we looked at one another, there was a palpable exchange of curiosity and affinity. I named this young female orca Toby after the helmsman's daughter.

Once I had used up my meager film load and was no longer looking at Toby through the lens, I tried using hand signals to mimic the way she moved her pectorals. She turned on her side and I did the same. When she swam, I paralleled her course. Yet again, I was in conversation with a nonhuman intelligence in a remote ocean. My singing had again attracted a huge alien. Mimicry allowed us to say, "I see you, and I see that you see me." And this conversation while simple is the most basic opening to further relationship. It co-communicates that we are not members of species that are merely instinct driven. We are individuals who perceive and have empathy for one another.

I started to hum again, and she rose from the depths with a huge white-and-pink jellyfish in her mouth. She swam back and forth, clearly showing her prize off to me, perhaps offering it as a gift, just as Didi had done with the sea cucumber. I thought furiously of some way to reciprocate her offering, but with the camera in my hand and the dry suit severely limiting my motion, I could do nothing. I wished I'd had the Red Mickey, our windup fish. Toward the end of the swim, two other orcas appeared below us but were so deep that they were almost at the limit of visibility. They were perhaps looking after their adventurous pod mate.

As the last glow of the sun faded to midnight blue, I got back on the boat. Toby surfaced very nearby a couple of times, but once I was out of the water, she went off to check out a sailboat a short distance away.

Over the next few days, we continued filming on the surface, always ready to drop into the water if opportunity presented itself. One of those dives almost proved fatal. The air temperature had dropped below freezing. Blotches of pale blue broke the leaden skies. A subpod of five orcas approached our boat, closer than any previous group. By their behavior and the presence of shrieking sea gulls, we judged they were chasing a school of herring. I wanted to get footage of their remarkable coordinated hunting behavior, so I slipped into the water and began swimming toward the feeding group.

A young male broke away from the adults, swam over, and stopped directly in front of the camera. Rotating his head, he looked at the camera dome first with one eye, then the other. It's possible he could see himself reflected in the dome port. Although obviously a calf, he had a girth far larger than I could have circled with my arms. He hesitated, moved forward almost to the point of touching the dome, hung in the water an arm's length away, then broke off and swam back to his pod mates. This youngster had come even closer than Toby, and the experience was electrifying and slightly unnerving. I'd felt myself in his shadow; his eye, wide open and as big as a half dollar, was reddish, a sign of excitement or aggression.

As I swam back into the midst of the orca family, they began circling me. I bent at the waist, lifted my fins above me, and used the weight of my legs to drive me underwater, intending to stop just below the surface. As the whales circled, I lifted the camera to my eye and began filming. Nice stuff, the orca beside me, the orca above me, the orca over my head.

The orca family then moved off and dived into the herring. I wanted that feeding shot and swam toward the location only fifty yards away where I could see them lunging and diving. Swimming with my head in the water for speed then coming upright in the water and kicking hard to get a little elevation, I could spot curving black dorsals and tail flukes at the surface.

Then all signs of the orcas disappeared. I put my head in the water. For a few seconds, there was nothing but gray green gloom. Suddenly they appeared, white chevrons blazing, heading for me at high speed. As they closed in, the adults veered off slightly to pass above or to my left. But one held course straight for me. It all happened in perhaps six seconds. He came on. I raised the camera and triggered the mechanism. It made a slight whirring sound in the water. The orca broke off his charge less than six feet from me, cutting straight over my head.

I swam back to the surface utterly drained. The approach might have been a threat display, maybe the stereotypical behavior of young males of all species, a game of chicken. It didn't matter. This young orca had gone from curious to rambunctious, and even if he had only playful intentions, he posed a lethal threat. I got out of the water.

A day later, we flew home to San Francisco via Oslo and London. Leaving Toby and the other orca of Tysfjord brought a great sense of loss, as though I were losing a lover.

~ 7 ~

Auschwitz for Dolphins

As the scope of my filmmaking work expanded, taking me to islands and oceans around the world, there were always a few constants on my itinerary. One was a yearly trip back to the white sands of the Bahamas, to renew and maintain my relationship with the pod of spotted dolphins, especially with particular individuals and to continue documenting this non-human society and culture. The other place to which I kept returning was Taiji, Japan.

It's a familiar name today after a series of television films, news reports, and Internet publicity. In 2003, National Geographic Television International released my film *When Dolphins Cry*. In 2005, NATURE on PBS aired *The Dolphin Defender*, which had a long sequence on the hunting of dolphins in Taiji and Futo. We were also covered in the PBS program *The State of the Ocean's Animals*, beautifully narrated by Matt Damon. Then came a filmic tsunami—Louie Psihoyos's *The Cove*. Ric O'Barry, who had been on our first dolphin trip in 1978, was the star of the film. *The Cove* won pretty much every film competition into which it was entered, including the Academy Awards in 2010. It's hard to imagine a greater avalanche of publicity depicting the business of killing dolphins in Japan.

And yet, as of this writing, the slaughter continues. The films mentioned may ultimately play a part in ending this ghastly business. For years I had thought that if enough publicity were brought to bear, if enough protest letters came in, Japan would bring an end to the killings. Now I realize that it is unrealistic to imagine that even such massive publicity would force a sovereign country to alter its national policy.

Author and Larry Curtis prepare to connect to the world via computer and sat phone

It is ironic that this huge publicity effort may actually impede or delay the results we so devoutly work toward. The Japanese cannot allow themselves to be seen kowtowing to a bunch of Western filmmakers. The loss of face would be intolerable. To some degree, they may feel they have to continue dolphin hunting and whaling just to show the world enviros can't kick them around. So I began looking for other stratagems.

Images of the slaughter of the dolphins and small whales at Taiji are never far from my thoughts. Working with the footage in the editing process reinforces the original experience of witnessing the dolphin killings and reveals details I was not aware of while shooting the scene. So it's always with a vivid sense of dread and foreboding that I step into that series of metal tubes that transport me from the benign world of my home in Florida across America and then five thousand miles of the Pacific to Osaka.

In the course of my travels to Japan, I'd come to realize that saving local fisheries and providing dolphin meat for Japanese tables weren't the only motives for the annual drive hunts at Taiji and elsewhere. A major part of the incentive to local fishermen to pursue and kill dolphins is cash put on the table by international dolphin traffickers who come to Taiji to pick out "show-quality" dolphins. They pay enormous amounts, as much as $150,000 for a dolphin trained in Taiji. The service includes trainers who will accompany the locally trained dolphin to its final destination in one of the many dolphinaria in Japan, as well as to China, Korea, French Polynesia, Turkey and Egypt. For dolphins, this must be the equivalent of an alien abduction. The captive dolphins eventually end up in a cement tank performing for fish in aquarium shows and "swim-with-dolphins" programs around the world.

One of my earlier trips to Taiji had put me on the scene of an unusual form of dolphin trafficking. In January 1988, while filming in Hawaii, I had learned that Dr. Jay Sweeney, a well-known marine mammal vet, was staying at a hotel on the Big Island where he ran a swim-with-dolphins business. Sweeney had provided me information during the dolphin die-off the previous year. I called him and set up a dinner. I didn't have anything specific in mind—maybe to learn more about the possible causes of that catastrophic event.

I knew that Sweeney was one of the leading captors of dolphins for aquariums and marine mammal shows worldwide. He had supplied dolphins to the Miami Seaquarium, Sea-World, and the Dolphin Quest program at what was then the Hilton Waikoloa on Hawaii's Big Island—even to a nightclub in Switzerland. That made us antagonists but I thought I'd just act friendly and see what I could learn. When I told him about being at Iki and Taiji in the late 1970s and early 1980s, he shocked me by saying that he was headed to Taiji in April. The only reason for such a trip would be to obtain dolphins for captivity. I couldn't believe he would tell me this. Didn't he know who I was? That I absolutely opposed dolphin captivity?

I expressed only polite interest in this information but determined to be there when he arrived to document this aspect of the hunts in Japan. I timed my visit to Taiji based on the information Sweeney had given me, and arrived on the scene to find him leading a team of what appeared to be Americans in wrestling two Risso's dolphins out of a sea pen in the harbor at Taiji-town.

I started filming and was approached by a no-nonsense military type who asked me to stop. I kept rolling while asking him by what authority he made this request. He admitted he had no authority in Japan, so I told him to stop interfering with my legitimate journalistic work. I half expected a karate chop to the neck, but to my great surprise, he just walked away.

The capture team, including an extremely attractive blonde wearing a SeaWorld T-shirt, wrestled the poor dolphins into a sling, hauled them out of the water, and put them in a truck that was driven to Nagoya, where they were flown to Kaneohe Naval Air Station in Hawaii.

Japanese trainers assisting in the operation told me the dolphins were destined for a highly secret U.S. Navy program. The Navy would observe and test the dolphins to find out how they move so rapidly and effortlessly through the water, how they use sonar and other characteristics that would enable us to improve our submarine warfare capabilities.

As this was going on, Sweeney approached and begged me to stop filming. He did the usual stupid trick of putting his hand over the camera lens, which is tantamount to admission of guilt. But he couldn't stop me. Sweeney asked me how I had known to come to Taiji on that day. I thought of telling him he had told me he'd be there during our recent dinner in Hawaii. That would have given me the satisfaction of making him feel like a fool. But I took another tack. "Jay, we have people within your organization who pretty well keep us posted on everything you do," I said with a straight face. He froze, utterly perplexed. Of course, I was fabricating this story to put the worry into him that he had a mole in his company. I loved it.

Some months later, I was told Sweeney would be interviewed by KCBS television in San Francisco about his role in the captivity industry. A reporter called me in advance and asked for the footage I'd shot of the capture at Taiji. During the interview with Sweeney, the reporter asked him about taking dolphins from the Japanese drive fisheries. Not only did he deny taking dolphins from the dolphin hunters; he also flatly denied ever being in Japan.

At this point, the reporter punched the Play button on the video recorder and up popped those lovely shots I'd taken of Jay directing the placement of dolphins in the back of a truck and then the bit where he placed his hand over the camera lens. As the footage ran on a monitor, Sweeney was reduced to tears. Those who rip dolphins from their families and pod mates should be made of sterner stuff.

Two or three years later, in the baggage claim area at San Francisco Airport, I ran into the Navy fellow who had asked me to stop filming. We were both perfectly friendly. There was nothing to be gained by showing my contempt. As we waited for our bags, we chatted and I asked him, "How are those dolphins from Taiji doing?"

"Great," he replied instantly. Then corrected himself "Well, one of them died."

So a 50 percent mortality rate was "great." It showed me the value these people place on the lives of dolphins. To them, dolphins are mere commodities.

I never learned anything more about the Navy's work with dolphins. Jay Sweeney continued to participate in the capture of dolphins through an operation called Dolphin Quest that allows people to swim with dolphins for a hefty price. Dolphin Quests were set up in Bermuda, on the islands of Oahu and Hawaii, and at the International Spa and Resort on the island of Moorea in French Polynesia.

Exposing Jay Sweeney was a small triumph, but it didn't change anything. Year after year, I would leave Taiji frustrated at having made so little headway in stopping the hunts. It wasn't until 2001 that we made real progress—thanks to a fortuitous meeting with a thoroughly remarkable woman.

I'd been scouring the Internet for a contact in Japan—someone who had knowledge of the dolphin hunts and could act as my translator. Once outside the main cities few Japanese speak English, and the language barrier had hampered my work. I met Sakae Hemmi first via e-mail and then in April 2001 at a hotel in Tokyo. She ran across the lobby toward me, her face a beaming smile, her eyes shining with intelligence and friendliness, apologizing for being late. When I stood to bow to her I realized the enormous disparity in our heights. I'm perhaps a foot and a half taller than she.

Sakae was sixty-two years old at the time of our first meeting. I was fifty-eight, but she had enough energy to run me into the ground. We exchanged stories. She has no formal training in biology but is a recognized author on marine mammals in her country. I was surprised to learn that she had been working to stop the dolphin hunt for many years on behalf of Elsa Nature Conservancy, a Japanese organization.

As I recounted the events of my visits to Iki and Taiji in 1979 and 1980, respectively, and my encounter with Sweeney and the naval team in 1986, Sakae pulled out a notebook and added my stories to the voluminous notes she gathers in her investigative travels.

As in 1979, an image had precipitated my return to Japan: in this case, some gruesome footage shot by a Japanese cameraman in Futo, a village located a couple of hours southeast of Tokyo on the scenic Izu peninsula. Other than Taiji, Futo was the only place in Japan where the drive hunt was still practiced, although thousands of Dall's porpoise are killed by harpoon in the north of the country.

In San Francisco, CBS news correspondent John Blackstone showed me the video and asked me to provide context for it. The scenes playing on the monitor were beyond horrific: dolphins being forced into tight groups, then gaffed and pulled out of the water two at a time by ropes tied around their tails. They were then dropped hard on a cement pier. Some, still alive, were simply dragged up a cement ramp to the slaughterhouse where men with large knives walked among the thrashing dolphins casually cutting their throats. They hadn't the slightest sympathy for their suffering. As the dolphins died, they writhed and twisted. The butchers stood by smoking cigarettes. At the other side of the harbor, a swarm of trainers from several Japanese aquariums in brightly colored wet suits wrestled young and unblemished dolphins into slings, which lifted the dolphins onto the back of trucks that would take the stunned, terrified creatures away for lives of confinement in cement tanks, their families and life in the open sea only a memory.

These images broadcast on CBS News briefly brought the issue of dolphin killing in Japan back into the news, and I wanted to follow up with more film from Futo.

On the train ride along the Izu peninsula, Sakae and I discussed the footage I'd been shown by CBS News. She told me the footage had brought such bad publicity to Japan that a quiet word had been passed from the Japanese Fisheries Agency to the fishing cooperative at Futo that it might be a good idea not to hunt dolphins for a while, certainly not when foreigners are in town.

Although we didn't witness a dolphin slaughter—much to our relief—we did accomplish something hugely important on that visit to Futo. During her research, Sakae had made contact with Izumi Ishii, a man who had once been a leader of the dolphin hunters there. In her subtle and humorous manner, she had cajoled him into meeting with us. It was a unique opportunity to get inside the mind of a dolphin hunter.

It turned out that during a drive hunt just prior to the one I had seen on video, the fishermen of Futo had taken pseudorca, a species for which they did not have a permit. Ishii had protested and withdrawn from the dolphin-hunting business altogether. Anyway, that's how he tells the story.

We met Izumi Ishii on his boat in the little harbor at Futo. His family has a long tradition of fishing and dolphin hunting, stretching back six generations. Ishii arrived in a nifty silver Honda convertible that he drove around the docking bays of the fishing harbor like an Indy racing car. He's married, has two children, and an annual income of about 8 to 9 million yen, roughly $80,000, derived from fishing and serving as a fishing party boat captain for tourists.

Ishii-san sat cross-legged on a bench. He was smartly dressed in a checked shirt, windbreaker, and bright yellow gumboots. He's a handsome man in his middle forties with a brilliant smile. He maintains a Web page that provides information about his fishing business and some of his philosophy of life and had his own radio show.

Our first conversation with him went on for several hours and ranged over many aspects of the troubled history of dolphin hunting in Japan. Even though dolphins had not been killed at Futo since the infamous video had been aired, dolphins could still legally be taken, so the hunts could resume at any time. Sakae's research had proven that the financial incentive for the drive hunts came from two sources: the sale of meat and the sale of live dolphins to dolphinaria. About half the income from the 1999 capture came from the meat of about seventy slaughtered dolphins. The other half came from the sale of twelve dolphins to Japanese dolphinaria. If either source of money were eliminated, the cost of fuel, boats, and manpower would make the business unviable.

"Is demand from the aquariums an important motivation for the fishermen to capture dolphins?" Sakae asked.

"Yes. It is very big money. You can get 200,000 to 300,000 yen [$2,000–$3,000] per dolphin fresh out of the water," he replied. (Fully trained dolphins go for vastly more).

As the interview continued and dusk became darkness, Ishii turned on the boat's searchlight. Around us, perhaps thirty boats bobbed in the tranquil harbor. It was hard to equate this peaceful little inlet with the massacres that had taken place here.

Ishii seemed truly to regret his former way of life. "I don't want to kill dolphins even though I am a fisherman," he said. "Years ago we ate dolphins because we had to. It was difficult to find food to eat, but now we find lots of other fish to eat. Also, the dolphin shows emotions and feelings. When I go to kill a dolphin, I see it weep. There are tears in its eyes, and I cannot bear it. I cannot kill the dolphin when I see the tears running down from its eyes. And as its throat is cut, I hear it cry out."

The cries of the dolphins had reached the depths of the soul of the head of the dolphin hunters. He said he would never kill another dolphin. At that moment, radical change seemed possible.

Finally Sakae floated the idea that had been in our minds since she met Ishii-san. We had discussed it before meeting with him, and now judged that he might be receptive. Would he consider starting a dolphin-watching business to replace the dolphin hunts?

"In many parts of the world, people make a lot of money doing this business," she said in an enthusiastic tone.

Ishii's interest was instantly aroused and I heard the familiar phrase "*Honto desu neh?*"—"That's true, isn't it?" He listened carefully and seemed amenable to the idea. The prospect that we could convert a dolphin hunter into a dolphin tour leader seemed like a huge breakthrough, a real story of change and evolution of consciousness. Or was his response just Japanese politeness?

I left Japan shortly after that meeting. Sakae kept in close touch with me and Ishii-san. Creation of a dolphin watching business could be a huge step toward ending the capture and killing and perhaps not just in Futo.

In the meantime I was planning to travel to Taiji again that autumn for the annual drive hunt. This time, I hoped to take advantage of new media to get the word out instantly and powerfully. I set up connections to the BlueVoice.org website and the Humane Society's Animal Channel to provide voice feeds on what was happening in Taiji. BlueVoice had pictures ready to couple with my voice feeds. And assuming we got good footage, we could quickly transmit video over a wired Internet connection.

In addition to Sakae and me, our team on this trip included stills photographer Larry Curtis. Larry had paid his own expenses to get to Japan and was extraordinarily determined about stopping the dolphin slaughter. He was so intense that I worried he might not control his rage if we got into a confrontation with the dolphin killers. A punch-out with a dozen spear-wielding fishermen was not in our interest.

On the train ride to Taiji, my thoughts are inevitably yanked back to the terrible scenes of capture and killing I've witnessed in past years when pods of dolphins were driven into the killing bay. Sometimes, the dolphins seemed to escape the boats but were surrounded again and relentlessly driven into the bay. When the nets are drawn across the mouth of the bay, the pod or family or tribe of dolphins is doomed. I desperately wish I could simply do a commando mission at night to free these dolphins, but it wouldn't work. If I were to cut the nets, breaking Japanese law, I would be expelled and prohibited from ever returning to the country. That would end our ability to expose the slaughter there. In fact, releasing dolphins is a far more difficult challenge than most people imagine. The nets do not even reach the floor of the bay and the dolphins could easily swim out themselves. To my human sense of reality, the dolphins should be able to simply jump the nets. But they don't. Even if the net is pulled back, the dolphins don't readily leave. Sometimes I want to scream, "Why the hell don't you just jump the nets? Why don't you attack the fishermen and tear them apart? You have the power. You have the smarts."

But they never do. Whether they're bottlenose or Risso's or pilot whales, they just tuck in near the net that separates them from freedom and move slowly, rising to breathe, looking stunned. Males swim on the outside of the pod; the mothers with their babies on the inside of the circle, using age-old defensive tactics. But they have never been up against anything like this before. Their failure to avail themselves of routes of escape that are so obvious to us has nothing to do with a lack of intelligence and everything to do with being utterly confused and disoriented. Their sensory systems have never encountered anything like a net. The concept of confined spaces is utterly alien to creatures of the open sea. And the mature animals will never leave the younger, vulnerable members of the pod.

After arriving at Katsuura, the nearest train station to Taiji, we lugged our camera gear and personal effects up a long flight of stairs to a walkway that traverses the tracks and leads down into the village. I was struck by the irony of the station walls being plastered with posters advertising whale watching and images of friendly dolphins smiling from photographs. It sure looked like a whale and dolphin-friendly area. Outside the railway station, we saw newspapers describing the trajectory of a typhoon that appeared to be heading straight for us. Rain began to fall and the winds picked up.

It was after dark when we took a taxi to the Taiji Resort Hotel. Checking in, we were met with the usual Japanese politeness and smiles at the front desk, though we knew someone in the hotel would surely inform the dolphin hunters that *gaijin* (foreign) visitors had arrived. In the traditional Japanese-style guest rooms, hot tea and biscuits were neatly placed on the table. The wind outside rattled the windows.

Knowing that the dolphin-hunting season had begun, we took only moments to assemble the night-vision camera before making the ten-minute hike to Hatajiri Bay, the cove where dolphins are herded prior to their slaughter. We walked head down against the wind along the main street on the outskirts of town. Once there, we peered through the darkness, squinting through the pelting raindrops to see if there were dolphins confined in the bay. The video camera's night-vision lens penetrates only fifteen feet, so was of little help. We started walking along a path on the right arm of the bay, feeling our way carefully along the uneven stones in the dark. Larry glanced to the left.

"What's that? Oh God. It's a dead dolphin."

A young pilot whale was being washed around in the surfline by the waves. The action of the waves rolling the body against the beach scuffed its black skin, so the body was as white as a beluga's. The lifeless creature was a very sad sight, and its presence could only mean that other pilot whales were further out in the bay, probably huddling near the net line. We listened and, during lulls in the wind, could hear the breathing of the rest of the pod. I imagined the terror and confusion they must have been experiencing, facing barriers of which they could have had neither experience nor concept.

With leaden hearts, we returned to the hotel and prepped the gear for an early-morning start. The thought that we might be able to do something to stop the slaughter is the only consolation in these moments.

The next morning, we arrived early at the bay, as the sun's first light turned its waters blood red. The fishermen were winching the lifeless body of the white pilot whale off the beach up to road level. The rope snapped, and the corpse fell with a gruesomely heavy *splat*.

There was a shout. The fishermen had seen Sakae and Larry and gone apoplectic. They ran at Larry waving their arms and brandishing their long, curved slaughter knives. Their gloves were soaked with blood. As they ran toward us, they screamed, "No, no, it's prohibited"—*dame, dame*—"You can't take pictures."

"Get out! Get out! Why are you doing this?"

"Give me the film!"

Sakae tried to calm things down and bring them into a discussion. She told us that the dolphin hunters believed we'd come to Japan to take video of the slaughters because we make a lot of money from it. That, of course, is total nonsense. We're usually just able to cover our travel expenses. They have absolutely no concept of our feelings for dolphins; they're baffled that we would care about them as intelligent individuals and travel halfway around the world to Japan to save them. "Aren't there problems in America?"

As the fishermen pressed us to leave, Larry jumped in, saying the video would be on the Internet. At this point the apparent leader of the group made a desperate grab for his smokes. "*Intaneto!*" he said, as he lit up, looking really troubled. The idea of seeing the images of the dolphin slaughter on the Internet concerned him far more than if I'd told him this story would be on *60 Minutes*.

He then pointed to the fishing boat that is used as part of the slaughter process. It was backing out of Hatajiri Bay and turning toward its mooring in Taiji town. He spoke with urgency, even desperation. "Look, I have told the boat to leave. We are stopping our work. This will cost us money." He continued to plead: "Look at it from our point of view. We're in small boats. We put our lives on the line. We're risking our lives. This is our livelihood. You're interfering with our livelihood. If these pictures are released, the government could shut us down."

There's a notion that the Japanese are inscrutable. I find them to be extraordinarily straightforward. This guy was telling us the problems we were causing him. He was asking us to stop filming the slaughter because it would cost him money. He thought that if he could convey to us that we are jeopardizing his livelihood, we would just slap ourselves on the forehead and say, "Oh, now I see," and then pack up and leave. But really, he was telling us that what we were doing was working and might bring an end to the dolphin hunts. He was giving us incentive to continue.

The fishermen grew more agitated, screaming that they wanted "the film." Finally Sakae, who had remained cool and imperturbable until now, said softly, "We must leave. It's dangerous."

I phoned my first report to a voice-mail box at Humane Society of the United States (HSUS). It would be coupled with the pre-staged video and stills and go out on The Animal Channel within a few hours. The first Internet report brought an audience of unique visitors numbering fifteen thousand within twelve hours. In my report, I asked everyone listening to protest to Japanese embassies and the fishing cooperative in Taiji.

Meanwhile, the fishermen were nowhere to be seen. Sakae walked into town and learned from the woman running the dolphin meat shop that they were discussing what to do about us.

Day two was sunny. We monitored the bay against any attempt to kill the pilot whales. If they were going to die, we were going to film it. Watching a large male protectively circling the females and calves was agonizing for me. I had a slim hope that we could force the fishermen to release them but, in reality, knew they would eventually return with their long knives.

Later in the day, the boat used in the slaughter returned to Hatajiri Bay. It moved among the pilot whales, and suddenly, a man on the bow thrust a spear into the body of one of them. It writhed briefly and then went still. Moments later, the process was repeated. Both whales were then secured by rope to the side of the boat and dragged back to Taiji town for butchering. I filmed the entire process from a hidden position atop the cliff on the north side of the bay. What the fishermen were trying to avoid by this time consuming procedure was any grisly slaughter footage emerging from Taiji.

© BlueVoice.org. Photo from video by Hardy Jones

I continued to file audio reports. The audience built with each passing hour until we had reached three hundred thousand unique visitors. A tsunami of protest faxes and calls pounded Japanese embassies around the world.

And then the typhoon hit with a vengeance. That night I lay on my futon bed on the straw mat floor thinking of the terror of the whales. Sleep was fitful when it came.

On the morning of the third day, I awoke at 4:30 and, carrying my video camera, left the hotel alone. The killing bay was quiet— only the pilot whales' percussive breathing what I feared would be their last breaths. I walked along the southern arm of the bay to a point where I could see the incoming storm pushing huge waves against the rocky shore. Rain was falling almost horizontally in wind-driven sheets, but the temperature was mild.

As I turned back toward the road, a little white van appeared. It turned and the headlights hit me straight on. They knew I was there. They clambered out of the cab and started removing their implements of slaughter. Without thinking much about it, I walked toward them, camera running on my hip. They didn't seem to know what to do, but as I passed among them, I said "Sayonara." I'm not sure why. One of them growled something that Sakae later translated as "Sayonara, my ass. You know what we're doing, and you'll be back."

Back at the hotel, Larry and Sakae joined me, and we went out the rear door and took a coastal path to reach the ocean side of the killing bay. We climbed a steep stone stairway to a vantage point a couple of hundred feet above the bay. By the time we got there, the killing had begun. The fishermen were stabbing individual pilot whales, then roping their tails and dragging them to the beach to cut their throats and let them bleed out. I crawled out on a rock promontory and began shooting video. Rain was intense, and I wondered how long my Sony camera would hold out.

For a moment, I imagined what the pilot whales must be experiencing: held for days in confusion and terror, concerned for their babies and fellow pod members, then suddenly forced into a confined space and stabbed, roped and hauled to the beach to face their executioners. For most of the time, they would be conscious and feeling excruciating pain. The second rank to be killed would be hearing the cries of those first taken. Soon, the taste of the blood of their pod mates would reach those awaiting the same fate.

But I could think and grieve later. The job of the moment was to record the images. Looking through the lens puts distance between the cameraman and the horror. You have to focus and get the light right and make sure you have sufficient battery charge and tape to carry the whole shoot. But the massacre was registering in me, stored in a momentarily remote place from which it would erupt in later days and nights. I had watched these pilot whales for three days, and this felt very personal.

Suddenly we heard a guttural cry and several fishermen appeared behind us. "What the hell are you doing! You people are a pain in the ass," they screamed in Japanese.

Larry and I tried to continue taping, but our main concern became safeguarding the video we'd already taken. The mission of these men was to get it from us. We demanded to go to the police, but the fishermen laughed and said, "Fine; they're our friends." So we decided against that.

The fishermen carried long poles they use to prod the whales and wore hard hats that they swung at us. I decided the best way to get out of this confrontation was to move to a more public area, so I suggested to Sakae and Larry that we agree to accompany the fishermen down the hill toward the main road and the hotel, pretending to be following their instructions. As we descended, Larry and I discussed what to do.

When I got near the bottom of the stone stairs, I looked back at Larry. He made a signal that he would roll tape, and I made a break for the hotel. A young, heavy-set guy hit me with his hard hat, crouched into a sumo-like stance, and tried to block my way. Crossing the several hundred yards to the hotel in wet jeans was like running through glue. The fisherman kept trying to push me backwards. I made slow progress by putting out my arms like a bird drying its wings and then rolling off him to gain a few steps. I felt like an NBA forward working through a tough defense. My adversary smiled and yelled, "Ah, basketball!" We both laughed. What kind of confrontation was this? A few yards farther on, he hit me particularly hard with his hard hat, then apologized. "*Gomenasai*"—"So sorry." Only in Japan!

Larry caught up to me at the entrance to the hotel. We went through the front door like a running back and his blocker. Sakae followed. The fisherman ran into the lobby after us, screaming violently but we managed to get into our rooms and lock the doors.

It seemed apparent that no further videotaping could be done in Taiji. Outside our hotel windows, the typhoon howled, and we were not about to walk back into the hands of the fishermen. What was paramount was to get the video material on the Internet as soon as possible. This would not save the pilot whales now dead or dying in Hatajiri Bay, but perhaps we could thwart the next capture. We didn't know on whose side the police in Taiji would come down. At all costs, we did not want our videotape confiscated.

With today's technology—an iPhone, for instance—I could have shot video and e-mailed it to HSUS in Washington or uploaded to YouTube from Taiji. But in 2001, we had to get to a Hyatt hotel in Osaka to transmit via an Ethernet connection.

We got out of Taiji on the next train, and once checked in to the Hyatt, we turned our rooms into editing suites and began pumping videos to the outside world. I phoned audio reports to The Animal Channel and BlueVoice. Although we could not save the pilot whale families taken in Taiji, we had damning footage of the heinous nature of the dolphin hunts that I still hoped would bring an end to these atrocities.

A few months later, in the spring of 2002, Sakae e-mailed me in great excitement. She'd heard from Izumi Ishii that he would launch a dolphin-watching business in the waters off Futo. His inaugural trip would be that September.

The news about Ishii's plan dovetailed perfectly with a new film I was trying to get funded. Since 1979, I'd been providing film and video of the dolphin slaughters in Japan to news media and inserting short sequences into films about dolphins that I produced. But I wanted to do a full hour on this complex subject. The news that Ishii would soon begin his dolphin-watching business gave me the storyline I needed to propose such a film to National Geographic. A story solely on the brutal dolphin hunts would not find a television audience, but with the inspiring angle of Ishii's conversion to dolphin watcher, we'd have a really upbeat and dramatic ending.

The process of going from an agreement with the proper commissioning official at National Geographic to actually getting a contract is long and can be very stressful. There seemed always to be another level of approval required. Ishii's inaugural dolphin watch was set for mid-September. If I could not be on scene to cover it, I would have no basis for the film. By the day I needed to depart for Japan, the contract still had not arrived. I had to risk the entire shoot on my own funds and trust that the contract and money would eventually come through.

Sakae, Larry, and I traveled to Futo to film Ishii-san's first dolphin watch. Enviros arrived in Futo from the United States, Australia, and Europe for the big day. We had a warm reunion with Ishii, an amazing man, a very modern thinker in a traditional setting. He was willing to blaze a new ocean trail in a country where being out of step is not admired. And he is courageous. His beloved car had been vandalized by unknown fishermen who did not want to see dolphin-watching come to Futo. He forged ahead with his plans regardless.

Despite the prospect of a major breakthrough in our efforts to stop the dolphin killing, I felt emotionally flat. Only a large hot sake could briefly lift my spirits. I couldn't understand why I didn't feel more excitement and couldn't generate any real energy. Even before leaving home, I'd been feeling inexplicably fatigued for months. Now I was just plodding along, lugging my gear, pushing one foot after the other with no sense of vitality. I had no idea that something was fundamentally wrong with me and tried to ignore it.

On the day of Ishii's first dolphin-watching voyage, reporters and camera crews from all of Japan's television networks and major newspapers stood on the small cement dock in Futo Harbor. Ishii made a short speech in Japanese and then in English expressing his hope that this venture would open a new page in the relationship between the Japanese and the dolphins. He ended with the words, "For the sake of dolphins and mankind, I hope to have this dolphin watching be a great success."

"Amen to that," I thought.

At the hour set for departure, Larry, Sakae, and I, along with the international enviro contingent and a few television crews, went aboard Mr. Ishii's boat, the *Kohkai Maru*. So many reporters had shown up that a second boat had to be hired to accommodate everyone. We departed Futo harbor at 1:00 p.m. The weather was gorgeous: sunny, warm, and flat calm. We sailed for an hour and saw nothing but birds. We ran southeast and then north. Cameramen who had been on alert as we left the harbor took their cameras off their shoulders and lay down in the sun. I began trying to accommodate the idea that the dolphin watch might be a failure that would unfold before the eyes of all Japan and what impact this would have on our efforts to stop the dolphin slaughter. Ishii, captaining the boat from the flying bridge, was biting his lip. He stared desperately at the sea looking for the telltale glints off the oily skin of dolphins.

At 4:00 p.m., he turned for home. Although he normally masks his feelings well, there was no mistaking the stricken look on his face. I could only imagine the extreme stress he felt. He had invited the entire press corps of Japan to witness a triumph. Now it appeared he would lose face while fully in the spotlight. The dolphin-loving Westerners looked at one another. They'd come thousands of miles to see a glorious event that now appeared to be a pipe dream.

Then the radio crackled. "*Ishii-sencho.*" Ishii grabbed the handset for his radio and answered, "*Hai.*"

"*Makko kujira!*" came the excited report from the captain of the other boat.

Ishii's excitement exploded. "*Makko kujira, makko kujira,* Sperm whale," he screamed. And there it was: a single sperm whale rolling from side to side only a few yards from the press boat. Not only had we found a sperm whale, but it was friendly, spyhopping to look at the boats and their human occupants. Ishii went wild with joy. He began to sob and shudder as he watched the frolicking whale and the ecstatic passengers. The reporters scribbled, and cameramen rolled tape.

Ishii-san's first reaction on seeing sperm whale
Photo from video. © Hardy Jones Productions

"My God, we've done it," I thought. But the realization seemed distant. My emotions simply did not kick in. This was a miraculous event, a huge victory, something I had been working to achieve for years, and I felt nothing. I acted the part expected of me, congratulating Ishii and high-fiving Sakae, Larry, and the other dolphin huggers on the boat, but I couldn't lose the thought of "What's the matter with me?"

For Izumi Ishii, the day was a triumph. He had launched his business, become a national celebrity, and shown there was a new way to make a living from the whales and dolphins of Japan.

The footage we shot of that momentous day went into my film for National Geographic, *When Dolphins Cry*, which was released in 2003. International awareness of the dolphin hunts in Japan was at its highest to date, and though drive hunts were still going on in Taiji, I allowed myself to be almost optimistic that the tide might be turning.

Mr. Ishii's conversion to a dolphin-watch—not to mention whale-watch—leader represented a breakthrough. But I doubted it would have much of an impact on the dolphin hunters at Taiji. At this point, a new factor in the equation emerged: a possible way to stop the slaughter of dolphins. But this path depended on a horribly perverse fact, one that would have a very personal impact on me.

As elsewhere in the world, fishermen and their weapons are only one threat to the dolphins of coastal Japan. Ultimately, far more dangerous are the toxic substances accumulating unseen in the bodies of these mammals—and in those humans who consume many species of fish and any form of marine mammal meat.

As I delved into reports of levels of toxins in dolphin meat, I was surprised to see that studies had indicated dangerous levels of organochlorine pollutants in dolphins and whales at least a decade before BlueVoice began studies in Taiji. And Japanese scientists had written many of these reports, particularly Dr. Koichi Haraguchi, of Daiichi University, College of Pharmaceutical Science, in Fukuoka, Japan.

The presence of mercury and other heavy metals in the ocean food chain had been well documented in many places. Mercury itself is not so much the danger as methylmercury, formed from inorganic mercury by the action of anaerobic organisms that live in marine and fresh water systems. It is methyl mercury that is absorbed by living creatures. The higher up the food chain you go, the more methyl mercury accumulates.

During the 1970s, awareness of the high levels of mercury in tuna caused some high-end restaurants in New York to take tuna off the menu. But that awareness led to nothing, and when the issue was off the front pages, tuna was back on the menu. In fact, if you Google "mercury fish" you will find more than 9 million references. If you Google "PCBs dolphins," you get over a million links, the first of which is to the PBS site on BlueVoice's work.

When Sakae and I first met Ishii, she had brought up the subject of dangerous toxins in dolphin meat, which had been documented in numerous peer-reviewed reports and had achieved some press in Japan.

"*So desu neh?*"—"That's true, isn't it?"—"Last year I heard that there was a problem," Ishii replied pursing his lips and nodding his head up and down slowly. "When the media reported that dolphin meat was contaminated, criticism of the dolphin hunters increased, not only because of the cruelty of the slaughter but also because we are selling contaminated meat."

The presence of toxins in Japan wasn't a new phenomenon, of course. The region had a tragic history of mercury with the most egregious example at the village of Minamata. Symptoms include lack of muscle coordination, numbness in hands and feet, muscle weakness, neurological problems, and damage to hearing and speech. Extreme cases can result in insanity and death. The syndrome became known as Minamata disease. The disease derives its name from its discovery in Minamata in Kumamato Prefecture in 1956. The Chisso Corporation had released wastewater containing high levels of methyl mercury into the bay in which citizens of the town fished. One of the first indications that something was wrong in Minamata was the wobbling gate of cats that had eaten fish scraps. Cat, dog, pig, and human deaths continued for more than thirty years. The people of the town repeatedly brought the problem to the attention of government authorities, but the government did nothing to protect its citizens. A second outbreak of Minamata disease occurred in Niigata Prefecture in 1965.

There were more than two thousand certified victims of the disease, of whom nearly eighteen hundred died. It was not until 2004, forty-eight years after the disease was fully acknowledged, that Chisso Corporation was ordered to clean up its contamination. On March 29, 2010, a settlement was reached to compensate all of the victims.

The story of Minamata disease was traumatic for the Japanese people as a whole, and a commission was set up to monitor mercury levels in Japanese food. But the fact that the Japanese government had suppressed and resisted the facts surrounding the catastrophe at Minamata did not auger well for government restrictions on the sale of mercury-contaminated dolphin meat. In addition to allowing the dolphin hunts to continue, Japanese government policy put citizens who eat dolphin meat at severe risk.

And the risk was not confined to Japanese dolphin-meat eaters, as I would learn in a very personal way.

~ 8 ~

Not a Death Sentence

In the mid-1990s, I had started to experience fatigue. I'd always tended to work myself to exhaustion but would usually recover after a night of rest. But by 1997, I was waking up as tired as when I'd collapsed into bed the night before. I also noticed that my hands were shaking and my short-term memory was spotty.

I saw a number of doctors and tried to describe my symptoms in detail. None of them was much interested in what I had to say. None of them found anything wrong with me. One suggested the problem was psychosomatic. Then, on advice of a friend, I went to a chiropractor, Dr. Bob Culver in Los Altos, California. He was attentive as I described exactly how I experienced the fatigue, and suggested I submit to a hair analysis that would determine my levels of salts and heavy metals.

The results of the test were unexpected and alarming. I was high in cadmium and zinc, but my mercury level was literally off the charts, and he diagnosed me with "chronic mercury poisoning". Where on earth had I accumulated such toxic levels of this particular heavy metal?

One possibility can be dental amalgams containing mercury. But the form of mercury used in dental fillings is not readily absorbed by animal tissue. We then examined my diet—a diet I thought to be extremely healthy. I cooked most of my dinner in an iron skillet, searing vegetables such as pea pods, broccoli, and squash in olive oil. At least two nights a week,

I would slather a steak of either swordfish or tuna in chutney or oyster sauce and sear it in a very hot skillet on each side, leaving the center pink. I also ate plenty of other fish. My diet turned out to be anything but healthy.

Top ocean predators such as swordfish and tuna eat at the apex of the food chain. Because toxins bio-accumulate in the marine food chain, top predators contain high concentrations of heavy metals. As I ate my simple and presumably healthy dinners, I was absorbing high levels of mercury—high enough to become symptomatic.

There are two ways to get rid of mercury. One is to simply stop eating fish that contain high concentrations. The half-life of methyl mercury is 49 to 164 days so within six months 50 to 75 percent of the mercury will have been eliminated from the human body, though this rate of dissipation may not be true for the brain. I stopped eating tuna and swordfish, and my mercury levels dropped naturally. Another way to speed the mercury on its way sometimes recommended by doctors is to take zinc supplements that bind with mercury and eliminate it from the body in a process called chelation.

I took zinc daily and immediately noticed a huge increase in my physical strength and mental concentration. When I was retested nine months later, my mercury level was barely detectable. I don't believe I incurred any permanent damage, though it's impossible to say for sure. But if high levels of mercury are ingested by children in early stages of mental and neurological development, damage can be permanent.

I was relieved to have rid my body of toxic mercury. What I did not know was that when a fish has high concentration of mercury, it almost certainly is high in another class of contaminants: persistent organic pollutants (POPs) such as polychlorinated biphenyls (PCBs) and DDT—components of toxic industrial and agricultural chemicals. There was a time bomb still ticking inside of me.

In 2000, I married Deborah Cutting, an elegant, beautiful and smart-as-a-whip marketing executive who had spent a large part of her career in the record business in New York and London. We'd met at a presentation of photographs held by Getty Images in a huge stone room belonging to a bank in the financial district in San Francisco. The reception started at 5 p.m., and I arrived on time, the only person there other than some caterers. I grabbed a glass of champagne and sat down alone waiting for things to develop. A few people trickled in.

A woman walking across the floor attracted my eye. She sat down in one of the many empty chairs around the periphery of the gallery. Without making any conscious decision to do so, I found myself walking over to her, pointing to the chair next to her, and asking, "May I join you?" almost implying that it was the last empty seat in the building. She looked a little perplexed but smiled and said, "Yes, of course."

I took her to Tahiti, Rangiroa, and Moorea for our honeymoon. Thinking of her as a city girl, I was surprised when she took so readily to diving and filming whales from small boats in rough seas. Eventually she came to work for BlueVoice, and has proven to be a brilliant Web designer, stills and video photographer, logistics manager for our expeditions and the glue that keeps BlueVoice together.

Shortly after I returned from Japan in October of 2002, I began to feel a deep pain in the area of my left kidney. I twisted and stretched, trying to relieve the pain, but it only grew more intense. Eventually, Deborah drove me to the hospital where ultrasound revealed a kidney stone. It was extremely painful by then, and I writhed on one of those wretched emergency room beds as they pumped more and more morphine into me. It didn't ease the pain but made me feel as though I weren't in my body. The dissociation eliminated the distress of the pain.

High-tech equipment at the Petaluma Valley Hospital zapped the stone with ultrasound and that was pretty much it.

The pain disappeared. The next day, I peed bright red, which was a bit of a shock, but otherwise I felt alright.

Follow-up blood tests were taken and I was referred to a urologist who consulted me briefly, scanned the lab report of my CBC (complete blood count), and pronounced me good to go. If I had known then what I know now and even glanced at my test results, I would have seen something was seriously wrong. My red blood cell count was significantly depressed, and the creatinine value—measuring kidney function—was elevated. But no one at the hospital nor the urologist caught those very obvious indicators.

Although I didn't know it, somewhere in my bone marrow, a switch had been thrown, perhaps the result of my genetics, or contact with toxic chemicals; most likely a combination of the two. My immune system had begun to produce monoclonal plasma cells, millions of exact duplicates of a single immune cell that were crowding out red, white, and all other plasma cells, producing anemia and impaired immune response. Excess proteins were clogging my kidneys. The fatigue I'd so often experienced was the result of the low red blood cell count and low hematocrit (measure of blood's ability to transport oxygen). My blood didn't have enough red cells to carry sufficient oxygen to my body. When I look back on it, I'm enraged that the urologist was so utterly clueless. An opportunity to catch my developing disease early had been missed.

By that winter, I was feeling emotionally flat and unable to generate any physical energy. One afternoon, I threw a few apples over the fence at the top of the hill behind my house. The next day, I had severe pain in my shoulder and hip. Chiropractic didn't help. Acupuncture didn't help. In following weeks, I began to notice my heart skipping beats, making me feel as though someone were hammering in my chest. In January, I went to a cardiologist. A stress test showed I had very poor cardio for a man my age, which was odd because I did a fair amount of exercise. On the treadmill, I became winded quickly, and the test was stopped as I gasped for air. But the EKG and other tests showed normal results.

The doctor ordered no blood tests and was ready to prescribe beta blockers, a class of drug used to treat cardiac arrhythmias, but then changed his mind. He had no idea what was really going on with me and didn't look any deeper into what was causing the arrhythmia. I continued to go about my life, pushing through constant fatigue.

In the spring of 2003, I came out of the surf onto a small patch of sand north of San Francisco. The beach is no more than one hundred yards wide and almost disappears at high tide. Mount Tamalpais rises to the east, and except for a tortuous path, the way to the parking area on Route 1 is pure escarpment. For the past few hours, I hadn't been able to catch waves with customary ease, and even when I got a good one, cranking left along the face, I didn't generate the blissful feeling of being stoked. Even pulling off my wetsuit was a chore.

As I climbed the hill to the parking lot with my boogie board, wetsuit, and fins on my back, I could walk only a few steps before heart palpitations began. I was sucking in air as though I'd run a marathon, not deep breathing but desperate gasping. My shoulders and lower back ached. Instead of gathering strength from surfing, I had been growing weaker each time I went out. Dr. John Siebel, still my surfing buddy, friend now of forty-five years, and practicing oncologist, kept getting ahead of me. I told him to go on. I sat down on a rock, looked back at the beach I'd been body surfing for a quarter century, and took in the beauty of this wonderful place.

The marine layer of fog forming over cold waters off shore streamed through the Golden Gate to the south. But the sun still warmed the beach and the hill I was struggling to climb. Below, tiny figures ran along the beach playing Ultimate, a football like game, played with a Frisbee. Other sun-browned bodies were doing Tai Chi or walking tentatively into the chilly Pacific waters. Many of them were naked. Golden Labs chased the Frisbees but left Tai Chi practitioners alone; canine intuition. Beyond, the town of Stinson Beach rested at the foot of Mount Tamalpais like a snoozing surfer.

A sense of foreboding that turned to sadness overtook me. I was no longer able to climb this hill as I'd been doing for nearly three decades. I was not yet sixty years old. Something inside my body is deeply wrong, I thought.

In April, my primary care doctor ordered a set of blood tests, and when he called me back he indicated that my creatinine clearance was high (bad indicator) and my red blood cell count was quite low (an equally bad indicator). I was anemic but it was not something Geratol could cure. He checked my weight and found I'd lost twenty pounds since my last visit and immediately referred me to a kidney specialist. By an odd coincidence the doctor he recommended was a friend, Dr. David Connor, also a friend of Dr. Siebel. The three of us had traveled together to Mexico and French Polynesia on diving trips.

Dave was clearly uncomfortable. "Your urine protein is 8,000—80 times normal. That explains your weight loss. You're literally peeing yourself down the toilet." I tried to ask some questions, but Dave just said, "Go see John. He's the best diagnostician I know." My ears started to ring and my brain froze. Somewhere in the conversation, I heard Dave say the words "multiple myeloma." That did not sound like a good thing.

I made an appointment with John for the following day. To get a preview of what I might have, I went to the Internet and learned that multiple myeloma is a non-Hodgkins lymphoma, a cancer of the plasma cells in bone marrow. Monoclonal plasma cells (identical cells) replicate at the expense of other cells, thus driving down the numbers of red and white cells, hence my anemia. Whether coincidence or some genetic predisposition, my brother had been diagnosed with chronic lymphocytic leukemia (CLL) a decade earlier. CLL is a disease where white blood cells proliferate at the expense of the others.

My next Google search brought up "Multiple myeloma is an incurable form of cancer of the plasma cells. Life expectancy is 2.5 years." I stared at the screen. Reality seemed to scream. I could die—soon. I started composing farewell speeches in my head. Mostly I sat and stared.

My wife Deborah drove me to Dr. Siebel's office just south of San Francisco for the ultimate test for myeloma - a bone marrow biopsy conducted by thrusting a large needle into the bone near the sacrum. People speak of the test as horribly painful, but despite this and the gravity of the test, the procedure turned into a laugh fest. John doesn't believe in suffering and gave me sufficient nitrous oxide to start me laughing. My laugh was infectious, and pretty soon my wife and old friend were howling at my witticisms. Somewhere along the way, John jammed that huge needle into my back and got what he needed to send to Stanford University Medical Center for evaluation.

It would take a while for the tests results to come back, and meanwhile, I convinced myself, with support from Deborah and Dr. Siebel, to go ahead with plans to attend the International Wildlife Film Festival in Missoula, Montana in late April. It turned out to be one of the best decisions I ever made, putting me on the path to make *The Dolphin Defender* film.

Back in California, John phoned to say he had the bone marrow biopsy results. "I can tell you on the phone or at the beach. But I think you'd better come down to my office." My heart sank.

I spent the night staring at the ceiling of my bedroom, thoughts streaming through my consciousness like balls in a pinball machine, each thought setting off another. I'd had a good life, done more than most people ever dream of, helped save the lives of tens of thousands of dolphins, swum in the deep ocean eyeball-to-eyeball with dolphins, orca, and sperm whales. I thought of Deborah and my brother and sister being on the earth without me. I was sad for them. And then there was this subtle curiosity about where I'd go when I died. I remembered the myth that the spotted dolphins of the Little Bahama Bank were reincarnations of drowned sailors from the Spanish galleon *Nuestra Senora de las Maravillas.* Maybe I would reemerge as a dolphin.

On May 6, 2003, I went into John's office determined to remain cool, no matter the diagnosis. He confirmed the verdict, "You do have multiple myeloma."

I blurted out, "Oh God, no."

"This is not a death sentence," he shouted back at me. "There are good treatments today. I'll keep you alive until something else kills you." He gave me prescriptions for two medications: dexamethasone, a corticosteroid that gives a huge burst of energy and then drops you like a hot anvil, and thalidomide, the infamous drug that caused birth defects during the 1950s and 1960s before it was identified and pulled off the market. Thal, as all multiple myeloma (MM) patients call it, is an anti-angiogenic. It stops blood vessel development, especially cutting nutrients to cancer cells. For fetuses, that meant arrested development of arms and legs. For MM patients, it has the miraculous properties of suppressing the growth of cancer cells and boosting the immune system.

I began treatment immediately. Three weeks later, my blood tests revealed a staggering drop in the levels of monoclonal cells that are the product of myeloma. Within two months, this number had been reduced by 95 percent.

Over the coming months and years, I would discover that one has to be careful researching medical questions on the Web. I went back and read the article that had given a prognosis of two and a half years' survival time. It had been written in 1998 and covered research on patients between 1992 and 1996—three years before the miraculous impact of thalidomide on myeloma was discovered and prescribed for use. Included in the statistic were people in their seventies and eighties who would naturally have shorter life expectancy in any case. The Internet is a great source of medical information, but you have to be careful to know where the data comes from, whom it covers, and how old it is. Progress is being made so rapidly in some diseases—multiple myeloma included thankfully—that any data more than a year old might be totally out of date.

But those drugs have their side effects. A month after beginning treatment, I flew from San Francisco to Berlin to screen one of my films at the International Whaling Commission. Three days later, I turned around and flew home—fifteen hours of travel each way.

The evening after arriving at my home in Petaluma, just north of San Francisco, I felt my right calf. It was huge. "Wow," I thought, "I'm really developing some muscles in my legs." But then it struck me. It was not muscle development that was ballooning my leg.

In the emergency room at Petaluma Valley hospital they told me I had a deep vein thrombosis—a blood clot—that could be fatal if I weren't treated immediately. They did a Dopler test, a form of sonogram, and discovered I had clots behind both knees – a bilateral deep-vein thrombosis. Almost certainly they had developed during the long flights to and from Germany.

The irony is that the very effectiveness of the medications I was taking had produced this highly dangerous medical condition. The meds had killed a huge number of cancer cells. These cells went through my bloodstream, and when I sat, knees bent, on an airplane for long stretches, they collected at points where blood flow was constricted—at the rear of each knee. I spent a week in the hospital with legs elevated and then got up and walked out to attend my sixtieth birthday party. I was okay but will have to take a blood thinner for the rest of my life.

I now had a good prognosis. Myeloma was so far incurable, but it was treatable and becoming more treatable with every passing month as "cocktails" of drugs were proved to be highly effective. I was also learning how to deal with the medical system. Many doctors are highly able and dedicated. But doctors are also rushed, and they have agendas. One of those agendas is to utilize the highly expensive medical equipment in which their hospitals have invested. And some doctors are just outright screw-ups, as witness the egregious incompetence I had run into on my way to being diagnosed. Over time, doctor-by-doctor, I came to learn how totally I would have to be responsible for my own health and treatment.

One of the critical decisions a myeloma patient has to make is whether to undergo a radical stem cell transplant, which requires heavy doses of chemotherapy and a long recovery period. This procedure can lead to prolonged remissions but in many cases is ineffectual and highly damaging to the body's immune system. Such a procedure would have laid me up for a year. That would have meant I would have to give up all work and income.

The alternative treatment was the combination of drugs that was working so well for me. With such encouraging results, I wanted no part of a stem cell transplant and was able to turn my attention to making the film for NATURE.

~ 9 ~

I'm Still Here

NATURE wanted an upbeat adventurous film on my personal life story with dolphins. The film began with our initial discovery in the Bahamas and would carry us through twenty-five years of contact with the spotted dolphins, the efforts to save dolphins in Japan, and finally to the extreme dangers posed by environmental chemicals to dolphins worldwide.

Screening the archival footage brought me back to those mind-blowing days when we first met the spotted dolphins. I smiled nostalgically as I saw myself, so young and naïve, in that early film footage. I especially marveled at the idea of bringing the underwater piano forty miles out to sea to play music to dolphins. I had thought the idea ludicrous, but Steve had made it work. And the dolphins loved it. Reviewing the footage made me realize what an odyssey I'd been on for more than two decades and the marvelous things we'd seen, things I would hesitate to mention if I didn't have the film footage to back it up.

Now that I had a contract with NATURE and the first payment in the bank, there was just one detail left. I had to make the movie. And the first shoot would be very challenging. In November 2003, I would return to Tysfjord, to get footage that would enhance what we'd shot in 1996. That would require me to get back into a dry suit, a contraption that can be lethal.

Operating underwater in a dry suit makes me feel like the Pillsbury Doughboy and requires a tricky balancing act to keep the air pressure in the suit just right. You also have to make certain that the air in the suit, which is much looser than a neoprene wet suit, does not all rush to your feet. If that happens, you're irretrievably upside down, and if someone doesn't come to your rescue fast, you black out and die. Compared to 1996, my strength was much diminished. Rather than feeling that I had the wind in my sails, I felt as though I were dragging an anchor.

Was this really something for a guy with multiple myeloma to do? Well, what else was I gonna do? By the time I left for Norway, I had been on meds for six months and my remission was described by Dr. Siebel as "strong and stable." He had scheduled me to go to the University of Arkansas for Medical Sciences (UAMS), site of the Myeloma Institute for Research and Therapy (MIRT), when I returned from Norway. MIRT was, at the time, the most respected facility for treatment of myeloma in the world.

I flew from San Francisco to Frankfurt where I met Larry Curtis, and changed planes for Oslo continuing on to Evenes. Dag Vongraven, our friend and captain from 1996, picked us up at the airport and drove us four hours in a rented van to our hotel. By the time we got there I felt catatonic and just fell into bed. I worried the twenty-eight-hour trip from San Francisco had been so fatiguing that I'd be susceptible to common colds and flu or even that the stress of the flight would open the door to a relapse of myeloma. I took my thalidomide and dexamethasone and was asleep in ninety seconds.

The next day, I was up and ready to go. The dex gave me a huge boost of energy, and I recalled that the thal had properties that boost the immune system. As in my previous visit to Tysfjord, I found it remarkable that the sun doesn't rise until 10:00 a.m. and is gone from the sky by 2:30 p.m. But what was even more remarkable was that the air temperature was almost balmy. I helped load the boat wearing only a short-sleeved shirt. "This is mighty weird weather for November in the arctic," I thought.

Underwater filming in low-light conditions of the fjords is difficult. The black bodies of the killer whales provide no contrast against very low-light, black-green water. The images don't pop. What you mostly see are the white markings moving as though they were individual animals. But video produces a far better image in these low-light conditions than the 16-mm film I had used in 1996.

As Larry, Dag and I ventured out into Tysfjord, I realized how lucky we had been in 1996. There were no whales to be found this year.

"Well, what's happened is that the herring have made a great comeback. When you were here eight years ago, there were few herring, and they all ran into the fjord for protection. Of course, the killer whales followed them", Dag explained. "Now the herring are abundant and they're spread out over a vast area, mostly in Vestfjord."

Unfortunately, Vestfjord is a more open body of water and much more susceptible to wind and wave. To make matters worse, high winds and heavy rain were in the forecast for the following day. I've never had a shoot entirely wiped out by weather. That's the nightmare scenario for any filmmaker, especially when working on a limited budget.

Day one of the shoot was wiped out by rain. We had seven more days before we packed and headed home. I spent the day going over photographs of the orcas that had been identified in the Tysfjord area. All over the world, people are identifying whales and dolphins as individuals; no longer seeing them as a pod or a species but as unique individuals. This is very moving to me–a source of inspiration and hope.

The following day under gray skies and in four-foot swells, we headed for Vestfjord, passing two fin whales on the way. The

Norwegians still hunt whales, having taken an exception to the worldwide moratorium on commercial whaling that went into effect in 1986. It was unsettling seeing whales with a target on them.

We made little progress in getting video of orcas in the wild, but were gathering shots of me on the boat with the whales in the background—stuff you need to edit a film.

On day four of our shoot, I got an urgent message at the front desk of our hotel from MIRT: stop all medications. The medical team at the Myeloma Institute did not want my myeloma suppressed by meds so they could get the best results from the huge array of tests I would be subject to in Little Rock.

Two days after quitting the thalidomide, I emerged into the world I had known prior to starting treatment. A great fog and introversion lifted. My mind projected out into the world rather than being focused inward. I was myself again.

Author prepares to enter water with orca outside Tysfjord, Norway
© Hardy Jones Productions, 2005. Photo from video by Larry Curtis

We got slammed around pretty hard on that shoot but came home with the shots we needed. I had no glorious moments in the water with Toby or any other orca. But within the budgeted ten days, we did get the footage necessary to make this segment in the NATURE film work. I felt a bit of relief just to have survived the expedition.

Upon returning home I received a packet of instructions from MIRT to help me prepare for the tests. One instruction was that I needed to bring a one liter plastic bottle containing twenty-four-hours' worth of my urine. The twenty-four-hour urine test is a standard measure of how much protein is being excreted and how much of that is monoclonal.

When passing through security the x-ray brought my bottle to the attention of one of the guards. The guy eyed the container and asked, "What's this?"

"Urine," I replied, unable to think of a more elaborate response.

He hesitated a beat and said, "Medical thing?"

"Right."

He waved me through without another word. That was 2003.

I carried the container onto the aircraft in a soft bag, placed it in the overhead bin across the aisle from my seat, carefully checking that the top was screwed on securely, and didn't take my eyes off that bin the entire trip.

"How will the container deal with pressure changes," I wondered. In the end there were no untoward events bringing my package through and delivering it to the lab.

Oddly I felt a state of exhilaration while staying in Little Rock, taking a taxi from the Peabody Hotel into the research center each day. Over the course of five days, I underwent a bone marrow biopsy, a PET scan, an MRI, and a variety of other tests. One objective was to get some of my myeloma cells and analyze them for their particular genetic structure. We're approaching a day when drugs can be targeted to specific genetic properties in cancer.

Deborah flew in on my second day there, and we had a fantastic time visiting places like Doe's Eat Place, a favorite haunt of former President Clinton. I'm not sure what produced the euphoria. Getting a full workup for cancer wouldn't seem to be a fun thing to do.

The doctors at MIRT couldn't find enough myeloma in me to do the genetic assay. That seemed like good news to me; but not to them. They wanted me to stay off medications in order to induce a relapse so they could do the genetic testing.

On my last day there, I waited for hours to see a doctor who would sum up the results of all the tests and recommend a course of treatment. Eventually a doctor with a decidedly Prussian accent and attitude came into the consult room and spoke to me for a few minutes. He practically ordered me to prepare for a stem cell transplant "in the interest of your survival," then left the room. I sat there for another hour, then just got up and left. I had no intention of undergoing a transplant, and as for inducing a relapse, I thought, "Screw that." That was seven years ago.

Two weeks after leaving Little Rock, I resumed taking 200 milligrams of thalidomide and dexamethasone at high dosage levels. To get another opinion I set up an appointment with a myeloma specialist in Los Angeles who was aghast that I was taking such high doses when I was in a pretty good remission. He put me on 50 milligrams of thal and a much lower dose of dex. Some doctors believe a patient should take as much medication as is tolerable. Most today are moving to giving the lowest doses that will contain the disease and minimize the effects of the medication.

The lower doses reduced the side effects as I continued filming *The Dolphin Defender*. In February, I traveled to French

Polynesia to film the dolphins who share Tiputa Pass at Rangiroa atoll with hundreds of sharks. Again, I met friendly and curious creatures in the deep ocean. One of them swam over to me and danced in front of the camera, twisting to look at herself through one eye and then the other. It looked as though the dolphin was preening, but I think she was checking herself out in the reflection of the dome port. That is a sign of self-recognition, something once thought to be a uniquely human trait.

While I'm content with that conclusion based on personal perception and intuition, I'm delighted to know that gifted scientists such as Drs. Lori Marino and Diana Reiss have proven self-recognition in dolphins in a manner that withstands scientific review. Marino and Reiss used mirror self-recognition to prove that dolphins are self-aware. The story of this remarkable

Bottlenose dolphin examines self in reflective dome of author's camera housing 130 feet deep off Rangiroa Atoll.
Photo by Hardy Jones from video

work received substantial media play. In January of 2010, articles began to pop up around the world reporting a call from Dr. Marino that dolphins be treated as "non-human persons." The articles cited studies that have shown dolphin communication is similar to that of humans and that dolphin brains have many of the features and functions of human brains. In a statement that really pecks at the cosmic egg, Dr. Marino, Senior Lecturer in Neuroscience and Behavioral Biology at Emory University in Atlanta, said dolphin neuroanatomy "suggests psychological continuity between humans and dolphins and has profound implications for the ethics of human-dolphin interactions." Does it ever!

In May and June, Deborah and I returned to the San Juans to update our footage on Ken Balcomb's work. As we cruised across into Canadian waters, Ken spoke of the excitement of the late spring when the J, K, and L pods reunite after wintering in separate locations. "When they first return, we make a quick inventory to see who's there, what new babies may have been born during the winter, and who's missing. And usually there's somebody new and somebody gone."

Later in the day, we picked up a large aggregation of orca traveling from near Vancouver, Canada, all the way back to Friday Harbor, a distance of more than twenty miles. The whales were everywhere and in high spirits, playing, breaching, porpoising on glassy seas, and diving right under our bow. Snow-capped Mount Baker thrust into the radiant blue sky, providing a dazzling background for many of our video shots.

There was so much orca activity that I couldn't figure out where to point the camera. Deborah, on video two, focused on my confounded efforts to videotape our

Ken Balcomb's beloved dog Suchi attracts attention from huge male orca
© Hardy Jones/Julia Whitty Productions 1987
Photo from film shot by John Knoop

escorting whales. As I aimed on one area of ocean expecting a whale to pop, an orca mother and calf breached on the other side of the boat. I turned but always too late. This continued throughout the afternoon. Deborah's coverage of my efforts became an amusing segment in the finished version of *The Dolphin Defender*. The day ended just outside Roche Harbor as the sun set rosy gold on the placid waters while the whales continued their slow swim south. It had been a glorious day.

What Ken told us next was anything but glorious. As we reviewed footage I'd shot during earlier years, he named the whale on the screen and then said simply, "Deceased." One after another, I learned the fate many of the whales I'd thrilled to during earlier shoots.

"J6. He's gone."

"Just in a period of less than twenty years we've lost most of the adult males in the whole southern resident community," said Ken.

I was stunned and felt as though I'd been hit in the stomach.

"We've attributed most of the mortality to PCB levels in the tissues. Their immune systems are depressed, much like AIDS, so they don't defend themselves against common bacteria. And also their reproductive systems don't develop."

Virtually all the males I'd filmed during the 1980s and 1990s were dead. "J6, J18, J144, J10—all males. All gone."

Why were the males hardest hit? The answer is unsettlingly perverse. PCBs concentrate in fat-rich mothers' milk and are passed to nursing calves. The horrifying irony is that feeding the toxin-laden milk to the newborns helps the mother purge her burden of these chemicals, but floods the newborn with the toxins. This usually dooms firstborn calves. Later calves born to the same mother have a far higher survival rate than the first-born because the mother is carrying a lesser body burden of toxins.

Because males have no such means of eliminating the toxins they carry in their body fat, they suffer far more from these chemicals than do females. It is altogether possible that the resident killer whale pods of the San Juans will lose all their males and plummet toward extinction.

The sources of the marine contaminants are complex. Some of the PCBs clearly come from industrial effluent that deposited the chemicals in waters through which the orca travel, in the years before some of these chemicals were banned. But the deadly brews also arrive on the winds from Asia. Airborne contaminants cross the Pacific from China to North America in about a week. Salmon, on which the orca feed, also pick up PCBs from Asia when they migrate through the North Pacific.

PCBs and other toxic chemicals commonly used in adhesives, asphalt roofing materials, paint, lubricants, caulking, grout and in coolant for hot electrical equipment had flowed into Puget Sound for years.

Much of the contamination sank to the bottom and embedded in the sediment. But when the Port of Seattle decided to dredge the bottom of the Sound, they released these deadly toxins into the water column where they were picked up by currents and carried right through the waters of J, K, and L pods.

These orca in the Puget Sound–San Juans area are some of the most protected animals on earth. There are heavy penalties just for approaching them too closely in a boat. But nothing can protect them from chemicals that suppress their immune systems and even alter the amounts of estrogen they carry in their bodies. These high-on-the-food-chain predators living just off Seattle, Washington, have become so contaminated with industrial chemicals that their bodies must be treated as toxic waste.

I left the orcas of the San Juans with a feeling of horror that the species of which I am a member has become such an apocalyptic force on the planet. When I started my journey twenty-five years ago, I thought the fight would be against harpoons and catcher boats, against bad guys we could stop. But it was now clear the threats to dolphins and whales are far more insidious. These threats are threats to us all. And we are all complicit in generating them.

However, the news is not entirely hopeless. Indeed, the problem is eminently solvable. PCB levels in the waters around the San Juans, and even levels sampled from members of J, K and L pods, are declining.

PCBs and other organochlorines have been banned or brought under stricter regulation. There are less harmful replacements for all the chemicals that are so deadly. New legislation is being brought before the United States Congress that would totally restructure the way we deal with toxic chemicals in the United States. Europe has already enacted laws that are far more restrictive than those that currently pertain in the United States.

And lately there have been some good signs. Ken Balcomb has confirmed the birth of a new K pod calf. If it survives that critical first year, the Southern resident orca population will be 90, its highest level since 2006.

The spring of 2004 marked the first anniversary of my diagnosis of multiple myeloma. *The Dolphin Defender* was now taking shape as we edited the footage we'd shot. The rest was cooking in my consciousness in collaboration with executive producer Fred Kaufman and chief writer Janet Hess at NATURE in New York.

After learning from Ken of the dire predicament of the J, K, and L pods, it became imperative for me to communicate the truly ominous situation of the orca in the Pacific Northwest in the film. I could not make an "islands of paradise" film, depicting all the beauty of animals in the wild but failing to mention the extreme jeopardy in which human activities have placed them. You cannot talk about orca without including the terrible predicament in which they find themselves. That would be like writing about Nazi Germany in the late 1930s and leaving out the concentration camps.

During the course of making the film, I flew repeatedly to New York to screen the footage and rough cuts for Fred and Janet. When I said I wanted to introduce a truly alarming aspect to the film, I expected push back. But it never came. Fred just said, "Do it." And as the writing and editing progressed, Janet came up with more and more ideas for making *The Dolphin Defender* a strong conservation film.

In the end I got to make exactly the film I wanted.

The remote banks of the Bahamas remain apparently untouched. In June 2004, twenty-six years after I'd first made contact, I returned to White Sand Ridge to reunite with the spotted dolphins.

This reunion would be a major component of *The Dolphin Defender.* We also needed to document unique dolphin behavior, including interactions with human beings. More important, I wanted to capture on tape the essence of what it is to be a dolphin, to truly personalize and individualize these remarkable creatures so that the audience would develop a deeper connection to dolphins in particular and the natural world in general. But no matter how much extraordinary behavior we captured, the shoot would not be a success unless we filmed a reunion with Chopper.

The vast and seemingly empty shallows north of Grand Bahama Island where Chopper lives is the place to which I return to restore myself and be reassured that at least some dolphins and a small piece of the world are well. Each time West End on Grand Bahama Island recedes below the horizon, I rejoice that I am headed into that weightless blue universe where friendly alien species bound over the waves to greet me, where I have dolphin friends—no quotation marks. By any definition, some of the *Maravilla* dolphins are friends of long standing. The truth of that would be eloquently proven on the voyage upon which we were embarked.

Without this contact with the spotted dolphins of the Bahamas, I could not have more than an intellectual understanding of the "realness" of dolphins. Spending hundreds of hours swimming with them has allowed me to know they are as sentient, intelligent, emotional, and loving as any human. And this knowledge supports and impels me into the fight to save dolphins from the disasters they face

We headed north aboard *Ocean Explorer,* a sixty-foot motor vessel with a flying bridge originally built for deep-sea fishing.

It's a smaller boat than I would have preferred, but it's set up for film crews, and when captained by Gene Flipse, it's a very reliable vessel. Our team consisted of Larry Curtis, who'd been in the middle of the dustup in Taiji in 2001. He was the main underwater shooter, although I also carried a video unit. Deborah shot topside stills and video. Chad Roberts, an ex-military corpsman acted as dive master. Chad is built like one of those stone monoliths on Easter Island. Everything about him exudes competence.

Jon Ross who'd been with us in 2000 had housed a newer version of a Macintosh laptop in Plexiglas. The advances in computer software and hardware gave us an opportunity to interact acoustically with the dolphins in real time. I hoped that our expanding abilities to communicate might impress the dolphins.

The weather was hot and the sun brilliant. I felt reasonably fit but was no longer the diver I had been during the 1980s when I could snorkel dive to sixty feet, relax, and become part of the reef. I worried that I didn't have the strength to move against a current, and I didn't trust my body's ability to store oxygen for long free dives. But I was elated to be back in this place that I love so intensely. The following twelve days brought some of the most extraordinary dolphin encounters ever. The warm, calm waters made it easy to operate. Camera and divers could enter and exit the water without being slammed around by the swell.

As we cruised slowly over the white sand, spotters came to the bow. This was certainly not unusual. What was striking was that females seemed to be pushing their calves to the bow of the boat. They would prod the little ones until they picked up the pressure wave from our bow. This free ride seemed to delight the pearl gray calves.

After a short time, the mothers would slip off, leaving the youngsters alone. I'd never seen this behavior before. It was

Author attracts dolphins with finger rubs that produce sounds.
© Hardy Jones Productions, photo from video by Larry Curtis

obviously something that could only be done in flat calm conditions. But why would a mother leave her tiny calf? Then it struck me: the mothers were using us as babysitters as they went off on some adult dolphin business. Evidently they calculated that no shark would attack a calf so close to a large and noisy boat.

When we were in the water females brought their calves to us, allowing wonderful opportunities to document behavior on video. It was deeply moving to see the tender affection displayed between mother and calf. The little ones would roll around the mother's body, slipping over her back just behind the dorsal fin, then duck under her belly for a squirt of milk. There was constant pectoral touching. It was a tremendous privilege to be able to enter their world in such an intimate way.

On our third day out, the captain spotted surface-active dolphins at two hundred yards. From a distance, we could see only slight splashes at the surface. We approached slowly. Larry and I slipped into the water. Visibility was one hundred feet or more. The water was so clear I had the feeling when I let go of the swim platform that I might fall the twenty feet to the bottom. But the 82-degree, brilliantly blue water buoyed me, releasing me from the annoying constraint of gravity. We were working on snorkel, a mode that seems to reinforce the bond between human and dolphin—the common need to return to the surface for air.

A school of hundreds of blue runners, averaging six inches in length, had gathered under *Ocean Explorer*. Adult members of the dolphin pod seemed only vaguely interested in the fish. They played among themselves at distances of fifty to one hundred yards from the boat. Juveniles, aged three to six years old, mottled with spots that were just beginning to fuse, seemed to set up a perimeter around the blue runners. The young dolphins, alone or in pairs, pointed their rostrums at the encircled fish, occasionally loosing an intense blast of sonar. They appeared to be corralling the fish but not darting in to eat them.

The dolphins paid little attention to us. We could film from six feet away without disturbing them. This allowed us to determine which dolphin was emitting the sound blasts and document teamwork among the juveniles. We never did see the dolphins actually feed on the blue runners, so this roundup behavior was all the more intriguing. Perhaps it was a training session for the juvies.

At one point, a juvenile male bottlenose dolphin arrived on the scene. The spotted dolphins, significantly smaller animals, immediately closed ranks and surrounded the bottlenose. Spotters were on each side of the intruder, in front of him, and above him. The spotters had taken total control of the bottlenose by controlling his access to the surface, which he needed to reach in order to breathe. Once they had shown who was boss, they allowed him to hang around on the periphery of the action. It was a marvel to watch the social coordination of the spotters. The water came alive with clicks and whistles, and they acted with astonishing teamwork.

The weather was so fine that on several evenings, we were able to motor off the banks to drift in the deep water of the Gulf Stream and wait for dolphins to come out and feed. After dark, we set out lights that quickly attracted squid, flying fish, and a bouillabaisse of other little critters. It wasn't long before the arrival of four dolphins, and then five more, including a mother and calf. The dolphins were hugely excited, darting into groups of squid and leaping out of the water to catch flying fish.

It's an eerie feeling to descend into ink-black waters where the only light is generated by the feeble beams of your movie light. The imagination works overtime on what might be circling just outside the cone of light, but when I see dolphins playing and feeding, I'm reassured. They don't depend on light to see in this universe. Their intricate sonar will warn them if an unwelcome intruder is approaching. We filmed the dolphins for several hours and at 11:00 p.m. headed back onto the banks to anchor for the night. The dolphins accompanied us, riding the bow.

The computer communication system John Ross had devised produced some interesting results during the final days of the trip. I joined John standing on the white sand bottom in about fifteen feet of water. Dolphins lazed around us. It seemed a silent world except for the inhalation and exhalation of our scuba tanks and some barely audible high frequency clicks and whistles from the dolphins. But when John passed me the frequency shifting headphones, what had seemed to be a piccolo turned into a full symphony orchestra. Once again, I realized that for dolphins, it's not a silent world but rather a phenomenally rich three-dimensional acoustical universe, each sound conveying meaning, nuance, and vast amounts of information. Humans' inability to hear dolphins is one of the reasons most experience them as mute.

John transmitted two kinds of calls from the computer. The first was a synthesized call similar in pitch to an actual dolphin whistle but was not the real thing. The dolphins returned that call with a perfect imitation, just as they had in 1978.

Then something surprising happened. John recorded dolphin vocal output and replayed those sounds to the dolphins. They responded not with mimicry but with an original phrase as though attempting to carry on the conversation. Of course, we didn't know what they had said in the first place or what their reply was to the playback. I don't delude myself into thinking that we will somehow crack the code of dolphin communication. But there is a meta-message in what is taking place in those turquoise waters over brilliant white sand and that is that both species are interested in the interaction. That is the message and it is huge.

As we got down to the final days of our season, I had still not seen Chopper. I worried he had died. Perhaps he'd gone off with another pod, as males do in many species to preserve genetic diversity. I needed Chopper to make the perfect ending to the film and to show the extent of our relationship over more than twenty-five years. But more than that, I personally needed to see him fit and happy and still swimming the waters north of Grand Bahama.

Covered in a foreign legionnaire-like hat with cloth protecting the back of my neck and long-sleeved, UV-protective shirt, I stood on the bow carefully scrutinizing every dorsal fin that broke the surface. Miracles happen to those who persist. Late in the afternoon of our next-to-final day, four senior male dolphins cruised along the starboard side of the boat. They were playing casually.

A dorsal broke the surface. Its trailing edge was flattened. I knew in a nanosecond that it was Chopper. I ran a thirty-second video shot at the surface and then put on my snorkel gear, underwater camera in hand.

I yelled at Chad to gear up and follow me then entered the water on the port side and swam to the bow. With strength of younger days, I surged ahead and started making click trains and just plain yelling, "Chopper, old man, old friend. Yahooo. Heehaw."

Chopper turned and looked at me out of his left eye then snapped his head around and blasted me with sonar. My camera was rolling. Chopper charged over, inverted, and swam under me, then circled me whistling and clicking wildly, a mature male acting like the calf I'd first met in 1979.

I handed the camera to Chad who recorded Chopper and me swimming side-by-side looking into one another's eyes. I was elated. Chopper was safe, now twenty-five years old, a fully-grown male. I don't know how long we were together in this deep-ocean reunion. It was outside time.

Over a vast span of years, distance, and literally across two different universes, he recognized me. Did he remember the Red Mickey? Did he identify me by my elongated body shape or by the tone of my voice? I don't know. But no one could look at the video of our meeting and not conclude that he did know and remember me. So I'd delivered on my promise to find Chopper and bring back the images of this remarkable dolphin. We had a perfect climax to the film and an example of what special creatures dolphins are. They are not our equals; they're our analogs. You have to take a moment to think of the implications of this: what it means about the qualities of dolphins and other animals and what possibilities exist for relationship among the species, especially those with large brains.

As I say in the concluding remarks at the end of *The Dolphin Defender*, "What we've experienced so far is just a hint of what

Two old friends eye-to-eye again
© Hardy Jones Productions. Photo from video by Chad Roberts

could develop between two intelligent species, one of the land and one of the sea. One day, we may actually communicate with dolphins. But, until that day, we must be their voices."

~ 10 ~

Are Dolphins Doomed?

By late 2004, all the footage to make *The Dolphin Defender* was in the can. NATURE sent Janet Hess and the acclaimed film editor Frederic Lilien to Petaluma to work with me in finishing the film. Janet and Frederic had enormous energy and worked twelve-hour days. I had to retire for naps and went to bed early each evening. It was a little embarrassing because at that point I hadn't told them I had myeloma.

We premiered the film on PBS nationally Sunday, May 15 2005, at 8:00 p.m. Four million people tuned in on the first night, and to date, *The Dolphin Defender* (a title I felt drew undue attention to me but which NATURE believed would attract the most viewers) has been broadcast three more times in the United States and is now in international distribution as well as on sale in DVD. As I watched the film from the point of view of an audience member, I was amazed at its pace. *TDD*, for short, is nonstop action and covers the whole spectrum of the world of dolphins: the good, the bad, the magnificent, and the horrific. The ending when we find Chopper was intensely moving for me, and I hope for everyone who saw the film.

In succeeding months, *The Dolphin Defender* would win awards from The Explorers Club, Wildscreen, Jackson Hole Wildlife Film Festival, and a Genesis Award from the Humane Society. In 2008, I received a lifetime achievement award from the International Wildlife Film Festival. It was very gratifying to receive recognition that lends credibility to our work.

The winter of 2004–2005 was the darkest and longest I had experienced in northern California over more than thirty years. I had long recognized that my moods and energy are highly affected by the level and saturation of light in the environment. Even with the summer of 2005 coming, there was no promise of warm temperatures. Summer just doesn't work that way in northern California.

I loved the area but had had it with the cold and damp. Just a week after the TDD's premiere, I abruptly said to Deborah, "Let's sell the house. I think the market is topping out. We could move to the southeast, somewhere between central Florida and North Carolina."

I thought she'd dismiss the idea but she agreed immediately.

We sold the house in September and moved into a rental in Petaluma while we checked out the southeast coast over the following year. On a scouting drive north from Palm Beach, Florida, we spent the night in St. Augustine. We hadn't been looking at this lovely little town as a potential home, but when we awoke in the morning, we beheld a phenomenal beach close to the historic town—a beach not blocked by condominiums, as is so common along virtually the entire East Coast.

I looked out in the surf and saw youngsters catching wonderful rides on short boards. Then two dolphins leapt out of the waves in front of them. End of search. Deborah and I moved to St. Augustine in October 2006, into a home on - pure coincidence, I swear - Dolphin Drive.

Before we left northern California in the spring of 2006, my brother Barry, who lived nearby in Tiburon, a waterside community just north of San Francisco, died of chronic lymphocytic leukemia, a disease that seems to resemble myeloma but in which the proliferative cells are white cells rather than plasma cells. Despite the resemblance of the two forms of cancer, I could find no statistical connection between them and no genetic links. Barry had bravely battled CLL for thirteen years, and for most of the time, he'd done well. He and I had been great friends as well as brothers. We surfed together frequently, and our families visited often. We could crack each other up with a single word or glance.

With his passing, I felt the prospect of my own mortality more intensely, along with a renewed urgency to document the relationship between chemical contamination in the oceans and cancer in humans. To some degree, that effort became a way of filling the hole Barry's death left in the fabric of my life.

And finding new and ever more insidious examples of how marine toxins threaten the lives of dolphins and humans was not difficult. Developments around the world quickly showed we'd only begun to recognize the threat. I began spending hours in front of my computer searching keywords such as *PCBs, cancer, dolphins,* and *myeloma.* One of those searches led me to a report from Dr. Greg Bossart, a pathologist and marine mammal veterinarian then at Harbor Branch Oceanographic Institute in Florida. He had found multiple myeloma in five dolphins of three different species.

This was extraordinarily important information. It was not just the fact that myeloma had been found in dolphins. Dogs and many other animals have been diagnosed with the disease. Bossart's discovery made me realize that myeloma was not a barrier to my work or even something separate from it. It created an intimate connection between my own medical condition and the plight of dolphins. Questions emerged: Was there a connection between what caused myeloma in me and what causes it in dolphins? Could unraveling the etiology of myeloma in one species be helpful in finding its cause in all species? And what part did marine pollutants play in development of the disease in both dolphins and humans?

These questions propelled me to look into the genomes of both humans and bottlenose dolphins, genomes that are almost identical. Because they eat large quantities of fish that have varying concentrations of POPs, dolphins are leading indicators of how contamination in the oceans will affect mankind down the road. Dr. Bossart suggested thinking of them as sentinels.

I had met Bossart in the early 1990s, when I was producing the twenty-six part television series *Challenge of the Seas.* For the episode on manatees, we'd interviewed him at Miami Seaquarium, and he'd spoken of manatees that had been rescued after collisions with boats and brought to the Seaquarium for treatment and rehabilitation. One of them, named Maxwell, had not survived, and Bossart retained the skeleton to demonstrate the devastating impact of large boats when they hit manatees. Tears came to his eyes as he described his personal relationship with this particular manatee.

After moving to Florida, I contacted Dr. Bossart again, and he sent me a number of papers relating marine toxins to a variety of ailments in dolphins, myeloma among them. I was shocked at the extent and variety of disease in dolphins, as I had been when Ken Balcomb showed me the dreadful results of contamination in orca in the San Juans. I also recalled with a sense of dread what I'd been told by the man from the National Veterinary Service Laboratories during the 1987 dolphin die-off: "Dolphins and whales worldwide are in danger of extirpation—complete annihilation—from toxic chemicals."

It's impossible not to marvel at the coincidences that produce leads and connections of life-changing importance. I was doing so well on thalidomide that the Celgene Corporation, manufacturer of the drug, asked me to do a series of radio and television appearances during the June 2006 meeting of the American Society of Hematologists in Atlanta. I would be partnered with Dr. Brian Durie, one of the world's leading specialists in myeloma and chair of the International Myeloma Foundation (IMF). IMF provides funding for research and assistance to myeloma patients working their way through the daunting process of being diagnosed and selecting a treatment.

Dr. Durie is a friendly and enthusiastic man with somewhat unruly gray hair and a face that bespeaks tremendous humor and curiosity. He's a Scotsman, and his brogue is more than just a trace. We sat in a studio with a television camera pointed at us and mics clipped to our jackets. Every fifteen minutes, a new interview would begin. Some were television, and others, radio. Stage managers held up cards telling us the name of the interviewer and the radio or television station represented. Dr. Durie and I chatted when we were off air. I learned that his amicus brief before the U.S. Supreme Court played a key role in getting benefits for veterans of the Vietnam War who had been exposed to Agent Orange and were later diagnosed with multiple myeloma. Agent Orange was a defoliant that contained dioxin, a potent carcinogen and a chemical frequently found in stranded dolphins.

Dr. Durie asked me about my condition and said that my response to the combination of thal and dex was excellent but not unusual. I told him I still surfed and traveled widely while making films on dolphins and ocean wildlife.

"My, what wonderful work," he said with genuine enthusiasm.

"It *is* wonderful, but what I'm discovering in the dolphins I've been filming is heartbreaking. Many of them are loaded with pollutants, and whole populations are in jeopardy of vanishing from the seas. I've been filming orca in the San Juans since the early eighties, and they're so loaded with PCBs that their reproductive capabilities are seriously compromised and their corpses have to be treated as toxic waste. I've just come back from Hong Kong where pink dolphins get the full brunt of pollutants coming into the Pearl River estuary from China. Their mortality rate is unusually high." I named a few other locations where I'd filmed highly contaminated animals.

Durie was now looking at me in amazement. "Those places all have corresponding hot spots of multiple myeloma."

A jolt of electricity raced through my body. Here was one of the top myeloma experts in the world connecting the chemicals decimating orcas and dolphins with multiple myeloma in human beings. Again, the question confronted me: could I be a victim of the same chemical pollution I'd been documenting in marine mammals for more than a decade?

Durie was astonished to learn how much is known about toxic levels in marine mammals compared to humans. When I told him of Bossart's finding myeloma in dolphins, his eyes opened full wide. And when I asked him if he thought cleaning up the oceans could be considered cancer prevention, his response was immediate. "Yes, absolutely."

Probing further, I asked if he thought that investigating the link between myeloma in dolphins and humans might produce information that could lead to a cure. I was expecting him to say something like, "Well, let's not carry this too far." But it was just the opposite.

"Yes, I think there is a distinct possibility this could provide information that might allow us to understand the etiology of the disease and ultimately be part of a cure."

Dr. Durie and I agreed to stay in touch and share information. Thus was formed a collaboration that would lead to a worldwide investigation of the correlations between ocean contamination and disease in both humans and marine mammals. It seemed we were about to open a new chapter in the search for the cause of blood cancers. But that would turn out to be anything but easy.

The first task was to document correlations between high levels of toxic substances in the oceans, and clusters of multiple myeloma and other cancers in humans on adjacent lands. I decided to begin with myself and had my blood tested for environmental toxins. It wasn't cheap — $4,000. But if I was going to pursue this line of investigation, I needed to know whether I had high levels of persistent organic pollutants (POPs) in my own body that might have triggered the myeloma.

I contacted AXYS Analytical in Victoria, Canada, a company that analyses the contaminant levels on both the Canadian and American orca that pass through the Straits of Juan de Fuca and the San Juan Islands. They sent me a kit with a return Fed Ex package and preaddressed label. Getting my blood drawn and analyzed was a simple matter.

The report was three months in coming, and the results were staggering. I had hundreds of toxic chemicals in my tissues. The report showed significant levels of POPs, in particular, heptachlor, nonachlor, aldrin, mirex, dieldrin, and dioxins. But what really jumped out were spikes of particular congeners (subtypes) of DDE (a metabolite of DDT), hexachlorobenzene (a petroleum derivative known to cause cancer), chlordane (a pesticide known to cause cancer and banned in the United States in 1988), PCBs (the same chemicals found in declining populations of orca off Washington State), hexachlorbyphenyls, and PBDEs (flame retardants).

Not only were levels of some of the individual toxins high, but the combined total of all classes of chemicals, each of which could produce cancer by itself, was enormous. Beyond that, these chemicals synergize to produce effects greater than that of each individual chemical.

Where had all these chemicals come from?

I showed Dr. Durie the results of my toxics test. He acknowledged both the variety of chemicals documented and the very high levels of some of them. But he surprised me with the news that the levels in my body were not atypical in the relatively few Americans who have been tested for their toxic burden.

He then cautioned that just because certain values were 'common' in the general population didn't mean they were harmless, especially in combination. The very fact that they were common might mean the levels of pollutants in the American population were far more dangerous than imagined.

Our search for hard correlations between toxins in marine mammals and human myeloma would prove challenging in the years to come. But Dr. Durie's research work with the IMF turned up something profoundly significant about links between humans and dolphins exposed to toxic chemicals.

One of the extraordinary efforts undertaken by the IMF has been a genetic sampling of thousands of myeloma patients through a project called "Bank on a Cure." I participated in this study by swishing some Scope around my mouth, spitting it into a sealable container and shipping it off to a lab where my DNA would be analyzed. Thousands of other myeloma patients did the same.

When the results came back they went far beyond expectations and surprised even Dr. Durie. It turned out that a large number of myeloma patients have an altered gene SNP (single nucleotide polymorphism; *poly* meaning many and *morph* meaning shape); in other words, a variation at a single site in DNA. Nucleotides are molecules that, when joined together, make up the structural units of RNA and DNA and play a central role in metabolism. This particular SNP mediates the breakdown of dioxin, one of the most potent carcinogens on earth. If that SNP is compromised, dioxin and other chemicals accumulate in blood and tissues and DNA repair is compromised.

Some 10 million SNPs have been identified in the human genome. These variations in human DNA sequences can affect how we develop diseases and respond to bacteria, viruses, chemicals, drugs, vaccines, and other agents.

Understanding the genetics of myeloma is key to realizing the concept of personalized, targeted medicine — the application of medications that are tailored to the individual patient's condition. This approach allows use of the most effective drugs for a particular patient and avoids using strong medications when they don't work.

The paper describing this breakthrough, "Genetic Polymorphisms Identify the Likelihood of Bone Disease in Myeloma: Correlations with Myeloma Cell DKK1 Expression and High Risk Gene Signatures," was presented at the forty-ninth annual meeting of the American Society of Hematology in Atlanta in December 2006. The abstract of this paper is available at www. bluevoice.org/news_issuescontaminants.php.

The IMF research had led to a tremendous breakthrough, presenting a direct causal link between toxins and myeloma. For me, it went hand in hand with another shocking discovery published by Watanabe et al: dolphins and their kin lack certain genetic mechanisms involved in metabolizing type II dioxins and other potent carcinogens. This makes dolphins susceptible to catastrophic declines in their immune systems and leaves them open to a broad spectrum of diseases. With this knowledge, I felt my connection to dolphins more strongly than ever.

In the fall of 2007, Deborah and I flew to Cape Town, South Africa, to attend the biennial meeting of the Society for Marine Mammalogy (SMM). These meetings provide a venue for scientists from around the world to share information on the latest research on marine mammals.

I'd joined the SMM in the late seventies, when written and oral presentations ranged from the latest information on the songs of humpback whales to the stomach contents of dolphins killed in tuna nets and all sorts of information scrounged from the feces of walrus, elephant seals, sea otters, and even whales. In those days, discussing emotion in dolphins or other animals was not accepted. Virtually nothing was presented on diseases in marine mammals or levels of contamination in the oceans.

Perusing the schedule of the forthcoming meeting during the flight across the South Atlantic, I noted that much had changed in three decades. There were now workshops on culture among dolphins, something unimaginable only a few years prior. And a large part of the agenda was devoted to the impact of toxins on marine mammals around the world.

As we approached southwestern Africa, the video screen on the seat in front of me showed our course about to intercept the coast just below the Namibia–Angola border. Behind me lay the vastness of the Atlantic Ocean. It seemed almost unimaginable that human activities could have befouled and devastated such a huge area of the earth. Lord Byron once wrote that mankind had ravaged the land but his impact stopped at the shore. That's certainly no longer true. Human fishing activities have wiped out 90 percent of the large ocean predators, 98 percent of the some of the great whale species, and 70 percent of the living biomass of the world's seas. And in many cases, the remaining fish and mammals are contaminated with levels of heavy metals and POPs that threaten their existence both as individuals and as species.

Each year the impact of chemical contaminants on marine mammals becomes clearer, and at this 2007 meeting, the concurrent threat to human health would emerge as an ever more prominent area of concern. I saw our role as gathering and synthesizing this information into articles and reports for the BlueVoice Web site and for films that could be easily understood and make an emotional impact on audiences of millions around the world.

In Cape Town, one of the most beautiful cities on earth, Deborah and I attended days of seminars, poster sessions, and cocktail parties where we met researchers, scientists, and veterinarians who specialize in every branch of marine mammal science. The amount of work being done is staggering. These sessions demonstrated that scientists had measured the levels of heavy metals and POPs in marine animals from all over the earth; an incredible contrast to what we know about the levels of these same contaminants in human beings.

At a session on marine mammal medicine, I introduced myself as a filmmaker and myeloma patient who was investigating the incidence of myeloma in dolphins and other marine mammals. During one of the breaks, another participant introduced herself to me as Judy St. Leger, head pathologist at SeaWorld in San Diego. She told me that at least two sea lions and maybe a dolphin had been diagnosed with myeloma at her facility. (My notes indicate she spoke of a dolphin, but in our future conversations, she mentioned only the two sea lions.) This was the first I'd heard about marine mammals other than dolphins contracting myeloma, though I later learned that myeloma in sea lions is not uncommon.

As the rest of the meeting unfolded, paper after paper revealed a truly disheartening picture of the oceans. Each report was alarming and sad in itself. Putting together a mosaic of all the data showed an ocean ecosystem in catastrophic decline.

Susan Shaw, a toxicologist at the Marine Environmental Research Institute, presented research on northwestern Atlantic harbor seals in the Gulf of Maine. She showed that toxic chemical levels in the seals are as high as anywhere in the world, especially in pups.

A paper by biologist John Calambokidis reported a marked increase in harbor seal mortality in the Pacific Northwest.

One of the most interesting papers, presented by Michel Fournier of the University of Quebec, described an investigation into the exposure of lymphoma-B cell lines from harbor seals to various pollutants. The study led him and his colleagues to propose that exposure to pollutants can cause hazardous lesions in DNA, just as Dr. Durie had described in myeloma patients. DNA damage not only plays an important role in the development of cancer but can also be a risk factor for birth defects and genetic disease. There couldn't be a clearer statement of the danger of marine toxins to any mammal subsisting on contaminated fish.

Not all the news presented was bad. After the fall of communism in Eastern Europe, tough regulations on pollutants imposed by the European Economic Community began to be enforced in countries that had formerly paid no attention to industrial pollution. Levels of POPs in the Baltic Sea, for example, had fallen substantially.

Deborah and I left Cape Town deeply concerned and convinced that the most effective way we could convey this important information to the public would be to bring together all the data available into a single white paper written in layman's terms. We would expand that outreach by making a film for television about the tsunami of toxins entering the marine environment. It would be a personal story of my exposure to contaminants and my subsequent development of mercury poisoning and later multiple myeloma. But it would be a tough story to sell to television.

I spent hours on Google searching word combinations hoping to find data that would substantiate the connection between myeloma and contaminants in the marine environment. I found a jury verdict in Mississippi that established the link between marine toxins and multiple myeloma. In August of 2005, a jury of twelve citizens awarded oysterman Glen Strong and his wife $15.5 million in damages against DuPont Corporation for dumping carcinogenic chemicals in the bays where Strong collected oysters. He had developed multiple myeloma. I felt the evidentiary papers filed by the plaintiff could be a gold mine of information linking chemicals to onset of multiple myeloma.

But, my search was thwarted. Even Lexis-Nexis, a firm specializing in retrieving legal documents and court filings, couldn't find the supporting evidence submitted for the plaintiff, including tests to document toxin levels in the waters in which the oysterman fished, and on the man himself.

Though Strong won the initial trial, the jury award to Mr. Strong was reversed on appeal.

In May 2010, just after the oil spill in the Gulf of Mexico, I began contacting the legal firms that had represented Strong in the case and asked for help in reviewing the evidence they had used to win the original verdict. The secretary who handled my call simply laughed.

"You won't get any lawyer down here to talk to you unless you've got a case against BP. They're like pigs at a trough now."

But then came a breakthrough. I Googled up a report that had been written in 2004 by scientists (J. R. Jabera et al) in the Canary Islands showing multiple myeloma in a dolphin. The dolphin had been found stranded alive and loaded with POPs. The report provided a smoking gun connecting marine contaminants with multiple myeloma. Eleven PCB congeners, 23 organochlorine pesticides and 16 PAHs were detected in blubber and liver from the dolphin after it died. Jabera concludes "High concentrations of PCBs 153, 180, 138, and 187 found in the liver may have been associated with the hepatosplenic lymphoma (multiple myeloma)."

The connection between high levels of toxins in dolphins and multiple myeloma plus many other deadly diseases continues to emerge.

As evidence of the effects of pollution in the marine environment mounted exponentially, a question increasingly troubled me: how could I justify spending so much time and energy fighting to save dolphins at Taiji when contamination and disease were endangering dolphins, other marine mammals, the entire ocean food web, and humans around the world? The resolution of the dilemma would soon come from Dr. Durie.

~ 11 ~

Sentinels in the Sea

When I returned to Taiji in the autumn of 2007, as always, I traveled with Sakae Hemmi. We had long since become fast friends. I call her *Kagemusha*, "the shadow warrior." Her charm gets her almost anything she wants, most importantly, vital information from dolphin hunters, town officials, and local citizens—information that often is not in their interest to divulge.

Our focus on this and future trips shifted from documenting the slaughter of dolphins and whales to testing levels of mercury and POPs in both dolphin meat and in the people who ate it. We hoped to document the links between ocean pollution and the health of dolphin-eating people. Sakae and I began to test dolphin meat and found mercury levels ranging from high to extremely high. We were also able to test five dolphin-eating citizens of Taiji for mercury and found extraordinarily high levels of the heavy metal.

Without help from an insider, we couldn't hope to penetrate the closed and highly xenophobic society at Taiji to gather data on levels of human disease among its citizens. But Sakae, with her infinite patience and charm, found an ally. Mr. Y, as we originally called him to preserve his anonymity, sat on the town council. Earlier, he had learned (through channels I cannot divulge but you might imagine) that dolphin meat being fed to schoolchildren in Taiji contained high levels of mercury.

In response, he did something virtually unheard of in Japan. He broke the conspiracy of silence and, along with just one other councilman, went public with his opposition to feeding what he called "toxic waste" to children. His press conference caused a huge stir in Japan, and the schools rejected further deliveries of dolphin meat.

Then in his early sixties, Mr. Yamashita wore heavy glasses and had a wise and compassionate face tinged with sadness. He had a DSL Internet connection, very unusual in Taiji, and knew how to work the Web for data. He's a kind and gentle person, and in the Japanese context of never breaking the social compact, his actions were truly heroic. His efforts caused the villagers to shun him and his wife. For his wife, in particular, this was very painful.

Knowing this background, Sakae contacted Mr. Y with the information we had discovered about the mercury levels in the five Taiji residents we tested. He in turn passed the information to a bold young Japanese journalist, Hiroshi Hasegawa, who used it in an article published in the spring of 2008 in *Aera*, a leading Japanese magazine. In it, he described Taiji as a possible new Minamata. In Japan, comparing something to Minamata is a very strong statement.

Hasegawa's hard-hitting piece led to a decision by the National Institute on Minamata Diseases (NIMD) to test the citizens of Taiji for mercury and thus determine what harm might have been done by heavy-metal intoxication. Our tests of five Taiji citizens had led to testing of the entire town by a highly respected Japanese institution. I felt that this could be the big break we'd been working so hard to achieve. If the NIMD reported that people who ate dolphin had dangerous levels of mercury, it might force the government to shut down the hunt or at very least destroy popular demand for dolphin meat. But the NIMD tests would not begin for at least a year.

In the fall of 2008, I flew to Los Angeles to attend a fund-raising gala produced by the International Myeloma Foundation (IMF). It was one of those red-carpet deals with lots of star power. Veteran actor Peter Boyle had recently died of multiple myeloma; his fellow cast members from the TV show *Everybody Loves Raymond* and many other actors provided the talent for a wonderful evening of comedy with a serious purpose. I invited Ted Danson to the event to speak about the crisis in the oceans and introduce a short film I had done on my experience with ocean contaminants and myeloma. Dr. Durie spoke to the audience about the information we'd been developing and summarized data implicating heavy metals and POPs in a wider range of diseases. The evening ended with Dan Ackroyd and Jim Belushi supported by the Blues Brothers Band giving a performance that raised the roof as well as more than $1 million for the IMF's work.

But for me, the key moment came during a discussion that took place over drinks with Dr. Durie and Dr. Luc Montagnier, the French virologist and Nobel Prize winner credited with identifying HIV. The potential associations between chemical contamination in the oceans and diseases in dolphins and humans, especially where they had an impact on the immune system, fascinated Dr. Montagnier. When I mentioned Blue-Voice's work testing toxin levels in dolphin eaters at Taiji, Dr. Durie's face lit up.

Shaking his finger for emphasis, he said, "You realize that Taiji may be the perfect place to study the impact of heavy metals and POPs on a human population. It's a small town with little in-migration or ex-migration. There's no agriculture, thus no locally generated pesticides. There's no industry. So there are no confounding elements to confuse the study. Those people who eat dolphin meat have been found to have unusually high levels of mercury and other heavy metals in their systems." High mercury levels often correlate to high levels of POPs,

I reflected, recalling my early diagnosis of chronic mercury poisoning and then testing high for organic pollutants.

"Therefore," Dr. Durie went on, "any data on contamination levels in the people or disease levels derived from that contamination would surely point to a local source." And the only local source for hugely elevated levels of contamination would be dolphin meat and, to a lesser degree, fish.

In preparation for the 2008 meeting of the IWC in Santiago, we researched and published our fifty-eight-page white paper on pollution in marine mammals. One of the blockbuster reports we included came from the Faroes, a group of islands in the North Atlantic that compose an autonomous province of Denmark. The Faroes are infamous for annual pilot whale hunts called "grinds." Pods of these large dolphins are herded into bays and killed in the most horrific and heartless manner. For the Faroese, it seems to be a sport: villagers, including children, laugh and booze it up as they slash the throats of the terrified animals. Because dolphin meat has increasingly been shown to contain high levels of mercury and organic pollutants, health authorities in the Faroes conducted studies of possible effects on islanders who consume that meat. These tests showed that eating pilot whale contributes to learning disabilities in children and that there is a significantly elevated incidence of Parkinson's disease among people who eat it. They also produced evidence that large amounts of mercury in dolphin and whale meat attack the nervous system and interrupt signals that maintain optimal functioning of the heart.

The Faroese authorities had taken no direct action to protect their citizens from these dangers. But we hoped that the emerging epidemiological data might have an impact elsewhere. Because pilot whales are one of the prime targets of the dolphin fishery in Japan, we felt this new information might help persuade health authorities there to restrict the sale of such meat.

While in Santiago, we presented the white paper, entitled *A Shared Fate*, at a press conference and I was interviewed in the penthouse suite of the Sheraton Hotel for *The Cove*, a film that would explode on the international scene the following year.

Much of our traveling within Japan is by train. As always Sakae is taking notes.

© BlueVoice.org 2004

In November of 2008, I returned to Japan, bearing in mind Dr. Durie's suggestion that Taiji represented a special situation—not only as a place to end dolphin hunting but also as a microcosm of how ocean contaminants impact human populations. By now, I'd been traveling to Taiji over a span of nearly thirty years to confront the fishermen who kill dolphins.

November in Wakayama Prefecture can be surprisingly warm. The hillsides are covered with brilliant orange from the ripening satsuma oranges. As the train sped along the coast, surfers catching some nice rides came into view from time to time. I looked over at Sakae scribbling notes or reading documents as she does in virtually every waking hour. It was all so astonishingly familiar, so banal, yet I felt amazement that such a journey to so unlikely a place could have become a regular event in my life.

Being in Taiji, where dolphins are rounded up, taken into captivity and slaughtered before our eyes, is a brutalizing experience, and I have never hardened to it, though I can still work within a cone of mental detachment in order to get the footage or information that might end the bloody business. As the train clacked along the seaside route, I weighed what actions might really have impact. Yes, broadcast of the footage we took at Iki in 1980 had put an end to the slaughter there, for the most part. And many other villages quit the business, in part because the dolphin slaughter began to be seen as besmirching Japan's image internationally and in part because the dolphin populations had collapsed. A genuine triumph had come when Izumi

Dolphins are kept in abominable conditions in Japan, here in an underground amusement center. © BlueVoice.org 2004

Ishii transitioned from dolphin hunting to conducting dolphin- and whale-watching trips. Yet, despite the barrage of bloody images and successive avalanches of protest, the hunt at Taiji continued.

On this trip, we would also continue documenting the process of capturing dolphins and training them for export. Hunting dolphins for captivity constitutes at least fifty percent of the earnings of the Taiji dolphin hunters and is an essential part of making their business economically viable. China has generated a huge demand for dolphins, and the ones who swim the Kuroshio Current past Taiji are paying a terrible price for their newfound popularity in the Middle Kingdom. I know the dolphin hunters are livid that we enter their world with the aim of destroying their dolphin-hunting business. And I know there's always the chance that one of them will lose his self-restraint and use one of those wicked dolphin-killing spears against us, but so far they had only turned physically violent once. Indeed, one of the reasons I can travel there regularly is that the fishermen are constrained by Japanese law, and for the last several years, there's been a constant police presence when dolphins are rounded up. I certainly feel safer in Taiji than I would if I were trying to close down some form of hunting or a slaughterhouse in the United States.

At one end of town are the sea pens where the dolphins belonging to the fishing cooperative are held, trained, and then flown off to foreign lands. At the other end, only a twenty-minute walk from our hotel is Dolphin Base, a facility that conducts a swim-with-dolphins program and trains and exports dolphins for a hefty profit.

From the hallway outside our hotel rooms we can look straight down into a small cove where the dolphin and killer whale shows are presented at the Taiji Whale Museum. This cove is cut off from the sea by a cement barrier through which fresh seawater flows. A steep escarpment rises on the far side. The base of the cove is a grandstand from which customers can see the killer whale act. And behind those stands is a tiny pool in which Pacific white-sided dolphins swim endlessly in tight circles. It was not hard to imagine that such confinement would drive them to madness.

But the main purpose of this trip was to get additional specimens of dolphin meat and human blood to test for POPs as well as mercury. High levels of mercury had already been documented, but if we could also show high levels of POPs, and connect those results to epidemiological evidence showing elevated levels of particular diseases in human beings, we might be able to force the Japanese government to shut down the dolphin hunts forever.

Sakae bought samples of Risso's dolphin and pilot whale meat in town. Each time she entered the fishing cooperative to buy dolphin meat, I wondered if she'd emerge. The fishermen who run the store hate her, but grandmotherly women are highly revered in Japan, and she has always emerged with a package under her arm and a smile on her face. Not only has she acquired samples for testing but she almost always has some important bit of information.

We photo-documented each step of our process, including labeling, packaging, and shipping the materials to a lab for testing. It would take a couple of weeks for the results to come back. Meanwhile, we arranged to visit Mr. Y to update him on our efforts and solicit his help again.

He did not look well. Sitting in his living room, he told Sakae and me he'd been diagnosed with diabetes and a heart condition. I found it odd that a slender man who eats almost no sugar or fats would have diabetes. And I found commonality with him immediately. When one enters any Japanese home, the shoes come off and slippers go on. They don't make slippers large enough to accommodate me. They end up flying off my feet like projectiles or, worse, I trip and fall against fragile furniture. So I long ago ditched the slippers in favor of just wearing socks.

As we sat in Mr. Y's living room, Sakae plying him with questions, I pulled my socks down over my heel so that only the front part of my foot was covered; my bare heel rested on the floor. Myeloma and the meds I take can constrict circulation and lead to blood clots, so I frequently pull down my socks to allow blood to flow unrestricted to my feet. Then I noticed Mr. Y wore his socks in the exact same way.

Ah! He has diabetes and can develop circulatory problems and blood clots just as I can. In that instant, I felt an astonishing kinship with him.

As a former dolphin meat eater, Mr. Y had high levels of mercury. We'd tested him to confirm that. He'd eaten dolphin meat regularly for many years. He wasn't particularly fond of it but his father liked it and eating dolphin together helped sustain their father-son bond. Among the emerging discoveries about the complicity of heavy metal and POP poisoning in human diseases is a finding that high levels of mercury can damage coronary function. The metal affects the nervous system and causes faulty signals to be generated to and from the heart. Diabetes is a disease that is being more and more linked to high levels of POPs. Myeloma can be correlated to high levels of certain POPs as well. So Mr. Y and I share a deep, common interest in finding out what chemicals we have in our own bodies and in documenting their sources. I told Mr. Y about having had my blood tested for POPs, which revealed elevated levels of literally hundreds of toxic chemicals, and suggested that he might want to have his blood tested for those chemicals. BlueVoice would pay for the tests. He agreed without hesitation. Not only that, he contacted a dolphin-eating friend who is also diabetic and got him to volunteer for testing.

We would need more volunteers to fully make our case, but if we could find a Japanese lab that would run the tests, these two men would be a good start. But there was no lab in Japan that would handle the tests and in the end we were not able to test Mr. Y and his friend for POPs. There is simply no way within the Japanese medical system for an individual to order a blood test and ship it to AXYS Labs in Canada for analysis without a doctor's order. It wasn't that our efforts were deliberately obstructed. While being tested for toxic chemicals simply by going to the lab and paying for the tests was a simple matter for me, things aren't set up in Japan to permit this.

But just when it appeared we had hit a wall in our search for epidemiological connections, we got a break. Mr. Y, who had access to all Taiji town records, began burrowing into medical data at city hall. He found that in 2006, Taiji had the highest death rate in Wakayama Prefecture. For 2007, Japan's National Institute of Population and Social Security Research reported mortality figures in Taiji at sixty-seven deaths from a population of some 3,500 residents—a rate of nearly 2 percent. That's more than 50 percent above comparable villages of approximately the same population in Japan. An even more extreme mortality level was found in the village of Kozagawa, near Taiji, where dolphin meat is also consumed. The mortality rate there was eighty-two deaths among a population of 3,426 people, producing a percentage of 2.39. The overall death rate in both Japan and the United States is less than 1 percent.

Further supporting our hypothesis was a single, 8½- by 14-inch page detailing the diseases reported to health authorities in Taiji over the past several years. The number one cause of death was listed as "a form of cancer." And, for some reason, the incidence of cancer was significantly higher in age group 40–64 than for older age groups. Unfortunately, the document did not break out which kinds of cancers were being diagnosed, though the column "Endocrine and Metabolic Disorders" showed an incidence of 19.8 percent for those aged 65 to 74. Was this the result of the estrogen-imitating effect of POPs? Mental and nervous system disorders taken together totaled nearly 10 percent of the 40–64 age population. We might not have a case that we could submit to a grand jury, but evidence was certainly mounting that eating dolphin meat was causing severe health problems in Taiji.

The strategy for going forward became very clear—destroy the market for dolphin meat by revealing the levels of mercury and other contaminants in it, thus ending the dolphin slaughter and helping to safeguard Taiji's human inhabitants.

Back home, I awaited the results of our tests on the meat of the Risso's dolphin and short-finned pilot whale. Two weeks after I left Japan, my fax machine came to life and a seven-page report clacked out into the tray. The results, showing high levels of mercury and cadmium, as well as other heavy metals, were what we expected and constituted powerful evidence that dolphin meat was not suitable for human consumption. "Dolphins are not food" became a BlueVoice tagline. Depending on whether the meat was boiled or dried, the levels of mercury ranged from about 40 to 51 times the allowable level and for methyl mercury, from 10 to 19 times the allowable level set by the Japanese Ministry of Health.

Besides the heavy metals, the tests also showed elevated levels of PCBs and other POPs. Of course this finding was no surprise to us. The levels of PCBs in the dolphin and whale meat were 5.6 times higher than government regulations allow. While this might appear less dire than the quantity of heavy metals, mercury and methyl mercury have a relatively short half-life in the mammalian body, whereas PCBs persist for a decade or more. So if someone is eating food that contains 5.6 times the allowable level of PCBs or other organochlorines, that person will continue to accumulate these chemicals throughout his or her lifetime. The toxins will be stored in the fatty tissues and may contribute to altered hormonal levels. In men, they act as estrogen imitators, reducing sperm counts.

A study by the Japan Family Planning Association (JFPA) finds that young Japanese men are losing interest in sex in a nation already known for its low birth rate. A staggering 36.1 percent of teenage boys between the ages of 16-19 said they had little to no interest in sex. The results released in September 2010, found that 83.7 percent of Japanese men who turned 20 this year were not dating anyone, while 49.3 percent said they had never had a girlfriend. Kunio Kitamura, head of the JFPA, said the data confirms that younger Japanese men do not actively seek women and sex. The report goes on to say that nearly half the married couples surveyed had not had sex in a month. This would be a logical result of altered hormonal balance which can be caused by the ingestion of gender bending POPs and requires that testing for toxin levels be conducted on a broad scale.

By directly testing the population, we were able to conclude that dolphin meat eaters in Taiji not only have very high levels of mercury and other heavy metals but that the dolphins they eat also carry high body burdens of POPs. Thus, there could be no other conclusion than that people who eat dolphin meat accumulate high levels of chemicals that suppress the immune system and cause a wide spectrum of diseases.

While adults suffer serious complications from eating food contaminated by toxic chemicals, the greater impact is on children. If PCBs accumulate in a woman who gives birth, the child will begin its life with an endowment of chemicals that damage the developing nervous system, are carcinogenic and immunosuppressive, and can alter the levels of sex hormones. A new term has entered the lexicon. Babies are born "prepolluted."

~ 12 ~

Sharing the Ark

In June of 2009, I attended a new ocean-themed film festival in Savannah, Georgia, only four hours drive from my home in St. Augustine. *The Dolphin Defender* was a finalist. Dr. Greg Bossart, the marine veterinarian and immunologist I'd been in contact with since the early 1990s, was among the speakers. Bossart came to the festival from the Georgia Aquarium, where he'd recently become chief veterinarian. At the Blue Ocean Festival, he delivered new and devastating information.

Previously he'd found severe problems with pollution and disease in dolphins and what he labels "environmental distress syndrome," a complex of diseases resulting from high levels of pollutants that produce profound immunosuppression and open the door to a Pandora's box of new diseases.

In Savannah, Bossart reported that over the past two decades, some thirty diseases new to human medicine had been discovered. These diseases have appeared simultaneously in dolphins and other marine creatures. He appeared shocked and saddened even as he read his own report. The emerging diseases included forms of canine and phocine (seal) distemper virus, orogenital tumors, infections caused by new herpes and papillomaviruses, and brucellosis (an intracellular parasite that causes leptospirosis and fungal diseases).

Perhaps more ominously, not only were dolphins developing diseases previously unknown in their species, but test samples were showing they have developed resistance to a wide range of antibiotics. Evidence of antibiotics such as tetracycline, ampicillin, and even triclosan, the germ-fighting agent in hand sanitizers, have been found in dolphins in Charleston, South Carolina, and Indian River Lagoon, Florida. These antibiotics make their way into waterways from animal waste and as people dispose of them through the plumbing.

In his talk, Bossart noted that scientists at the Centers for Disease Control (CDC) consider resistance to antibiotics to be a critical emerging health problem for humans and animals. In nature, there should be no antibiotic resistance in dolphins. One of the CDC's main concerns is that MRSA, a strain of staphylococcus resistant to antibiotics, could develop in dolphins and ultimately produce antibiotic-resistant pathogens, or superbugs, that could pass from dolphins to human beings.

The original quest upon which Dr. Durie and I had first set out had expanded into what appears to be a worldwide threat to the immune systems of all top predators, including humans. Three months later, at the next meeting of the Marine Mammal Society, that impression would be reinforced.

In October 2009, Deborah and I traveled to Canada to attend the Marine Mammal Society biennial conference. The eighteenth biennial conference on the Biology of Marine Mammals opened at the Conference Center just outside the walls of the charming old city of Quebec. Environmental contamination and zoonosis were among the principal topics. The keynote speaker for a workshop entitled "Emerging Infectious Diseases in the Marine Ecosystem" set the premise of the discussion: unprecedented environmental changes are taking place worldwide brought about by urbanization, rapid global transportation, and global climate change. Among the most alarming consequences is the potential rapid spread of disease, including from animals to humans.

Previously, a bacterium, virus, or fungus commonly found in the marine environment would be routinely dealt with by the immune system of a healthy dolphin, seal, or manatee. But high levels of contaminants building in marine mammals are assaulting those immune systems, and what used to be routinely handled now becomes a serious, even deadly, health threat.

Interspecies disease transfer is not a new concept. AIDS is thought to have arisen through blood contact when a human killed a monkey for food in central Africa. The same is true for avian influenza (bird flu) and swine flu (H1N1). In an alarming development, diseases thought eradicated or pushed to the periphery of human society, are reemerging among marine mammals. Trichinella, the parasitic roundworms that cause trichinosis, once feared widely among those eating pork, is now found in ringed seals and possibly in walrus that have been forced to eat ringed seals owing to a decline in their normal prey caused by overfishing and climate change. Inuit people hunt walrus for food; as yet, it is unknown whether this puts them in danger of contracting trichinosis.

Brucellosis has been found in North Pacific minke whales and pigmy sperm whales. It's worth repeating that the combination of antibiotic resistance and zoonosis could lead to bacterial strains that would be classified as superbugs that do not respond to antibiotics and could cross the threshold between animals and humans.

Papers were presented on toxoplasmosis in polar bears of the Norwegian Arctic, about dolphins along the southeast coast of the United States with skin lesions, about giardia in right whales and streptococcus in marine mammals stranded around the British Isles. Sea otters in Alaskan waters have been found to have distemper, and the St. Lawrence belugas suffer from verminous pneumonia as well as a high incidence of cancer. Organochlorine pesticides have been found even in sea lions in the remote Galapagos.

What makes the situation even more ominous is that the warming of the world's climate is compounding the spread of these diseases. Organic pollutants bound for decades in ice are released when the ice melts.

Of special interest was a report by Carlos Yaipen-Llanos, of the Peruvian group ORCA, of an increase in diabetes in northern Peru among fishermen who eat dolphins. The increased incidence of the disease does not occur among members of the same village who do not eat dolphin meat. And diabetes among Peruvians is uncommon. So here was a connection between fishermen in Northern Peru who eat dolphin meat and our friend Mr. Y in Taiji, a former dolphin meat eater who now has diabetes.

In early 2009, Danish and Faroese health authorities issued a report of enormous importance. In response to new epidemiological data, public officials at last took action, recommending that the Faroese stop consuming pilot whale meat and blubber. Consumption of the meat declined sharply. For a while, it appeared the awful "grinds" had virtually stopped. But during the summer of 2010, agents from Sea Shepherd documented massive slaughters of pilot whales in the Faroes. So, as in Taiji, international opprobrium and even compelling medical findings seem unable to alter behavior.

Our 2008 tests on pilot whale and Risso's dolphin meat in Japan indicated that this meat was even higher in contaminants than that from pilot whales in the Faroe Islands. We immediately translated this information into Japanese and created pages in Japanese on the BlueVoice.org web site, in the hope that either Japanese health authorities or the public itself would follow the Faroese example. That hope has not been entirely in vain. Consumption of dolphin meat in Taiji and its surrounds has fallen. The Japanese government has warned women who are pregnant or likely to become pregnant to limit their intake of the meat of small cetaceans but has not gone nearly as far as the Danes.

During the summer of 2009, Japan's National Institute of Minamata Diseases (NIMD) finally conducted tests of Taiji residents for mercury. The first tests focused on the specific population of people who eat dolphin meat. I was certain that the results would document high levels of mercury in those who eat dolphin, and was hopeful that this might at last close the market for their meat. But based on my experience with the Japanese regulatory system, there was plenty of reason to be skeptical.

In May 2010, the NIMD released its results, and its report was typical of Japanese bureaucratic prevarication. Yes, said the report, villagers in Taiji, especially those who ate dolphin meat regularly, had astronomical levels of mercury in their blood and tissues. But, said the researchers straight-faced, there was no evidence of harm done to those consumers.

Clearly the NIMD's conclusions were flawed. Either by design or through incompetence, its investigators had not performed the standard two-point discrimination protocol used worldwide to determine mercury related health impairment. They had simply observed the citizens with high levels of mercury visually and determined everyone was fine. It is perhaps not irrelevant that the tests conducted by the NIMD had been paid for by the town council of Taiji!

After the results came in, I contacted Dr. Jane Hightower, a San Francisco–based internist famous for discovering the effects of mercury on patients reporting unexplained medical symptoms. She and I have communicated over the years. Her reply pulled no punches:

"There are many studies that confirm that methylmercury is toxic to humans and can adversely affect health in a number of ways. Of most concern with long-term overexposure are nonspecific symptoms, neuropsychiatric symptoms/damage, autoantibody induction, infertility, coronary artery disease, atherosclerosis, and elevated heart rate. These adverse effects have been seen with much less exposure than what has been reported in the people of Taiji. The Japanese government's approval of consumers' exposure to high mercury content as a result of a limited and inadequate study *has potential for disaster.*"

Our search to document connections between high contaminant levels and disease among marine mammals brought us back to California where researchers have found a large portion of the bottlenose dolphin population had developed skin disease. In the fall of 2009, we joined Dr. Daniela Maldini and her colleagues from Okeanis, a nonprofit operating out of Moss Landing, just north of Monterey. Daniela is a radiant woman with humorous and intelligent eyes and an unmistakable Italian accent. She and her co-investigator, Dr. Tom Jefferson, were taking biopsy samples of coastal bottlenose dolphins who travel the length of the California coast from San Francisco to the Mexican border. Many members in this population are affected by a variety of skin conditions, which Daniela believes indicate suppressed immune systems.

In an on-camera interview, she said, "We've found that over 70 percent of the dolphins have a skin condition that goes from mild to severe. Since these dolphins range from San Francisco Bay to the Mexican border, we're talking about animals that swim the entire central and southern California coast and are thus sentinels for hundreds of miles of oceans and beaches."

In particular, the research team wanted to learn whether these conditions might be the result of the presence of PCBs and PBDEs (chemicals commonly used as heat and flame retardants) and/or mercury in California coastal waters.

Bottlenose dolphin with skin lesions off California coast.

Photo by Okeanis.

We pushed off from the dock in the early morning. Fog lay on the surface of the water, limiting visibility, so we proceeded slowly in the chilly damp, until the sun burned through, warming us and making it possible to spot dolphins at a distance. The magnificence of Monterey Bay was revealed, bringing back memories of the many days I'd spent among squadrons of dolphins, blue and humpback whales, sea otters and myriad seabirds.

Tom Jefferson, a visiting scientist at NOAA, scrambled around the bow trying to line up a shot from his crossbow to obtain a small plug of blubber for analysis. The entire Okeanis team consulted the database of identification photographs and took exquisite care not to redart any animal that had been tested recently. Each sampled dolphin was photographed and correlated to a name in the catalogue.

We frequently had to enter the surf line to get close to dolphins feeding in the breakers. I'd never seen dolphins working in active surf so close to shore. Surfers, just in-shore of the feeding dolphins, stared at Tom malevolently as he aimed the bow, but someone evidently recognized the research boat and told his compatriots that we were good guys. The surfers returned to catching waves. Ultimately, three days on the water provided a good number of samples.

A remarkable thing happened on the final day of Daniela's research. A harbor porpoise was witnessed under assault by far larger bottlenose dolphins near the surf zone. Sixteen dolphins, all males, took turns ramming, chasing, and harassing the porpoise until eventually one of the bottlenose killed it. Two male dolphins, known to Daniela and her team as Avalanche and Medusa, brought the carcass over to the research vessel, evidently showing it off to the humans. The reason for such behavior is unknown, but theories ranging from food competition to redirected male aggression are possible explanations. Watching a dolphin or orca hunt fellow marine mammals is very disturbing. I've seen transient orca in the San Juans hunting baby harbor seals. It's the way of the wild, but my empathy is strong for the prey animal, and watching these kills is heart-wrenching.

Contaminant analysis is very expensive and the research team had to struggle to find the necessary cash and a lab to analyze the samples. As of this writing, Daniela and Tom's team is still waiting for some of the results of this research, so vital in determining the health of the dolphins of the California coast. Preliminary results from two of the blubber samples showed a minimum of 14 ppm of PCBs in a younger adult male, named Akeakamai, and a maximum of 40 ppm in an older male, named Ojii, who was at least twenty years old. Those are high values. For comparison, the U.S. Food and Drug Administration's action level for PCBs in red meat is 3 ppm, and material with PCBs above 50 ppm is considered hazardous under Canadian guidelines. So the magnificent dolphin who accompanied us many times during our time on the water was 80% of the way towards being classified as toxic waste.

Total mercury levels in twenty dolphin skin samples from Monterey Bay averaged 1.8 ppm and ranged between 0.6 and 3.6 ppm. The U.S. Food and Drug Administration guideline for ingestion of methylmercury is set at a maximum of 1 ppm. And it is important to note that blubber is an area of low concentration for mercury. Concentrations in other tissues are certain to be significantly higher.

Disappointingly, Daniela could not get the data on the levels of PBDEs from the dolphins she had sampled. PCBs have been banned since the late 1970s and are declining in many marine mammal populations, including the orcas in the San Juans. But PBDEs, just one molecule different from PCBs, are growing rapidly in the aquatic ecosystem in North America today. It astonishes me that there is so little support for vital research on toxins that affect the lives of billions of people around the world. But cleaning up these chemicals would be highly inconvenient; though not impossible.

In 2004, the European Union banned the use of PBDEs. Maine, California, and Hawaii have banned several forms of PBDEs. But other subtypes are still permitted and flow into the marine ecosystem. Researchers studying the breast milk of American women have found every sample to be contaminated with PBDEs. The study's results indicate that PBDE concentrations in the breast milk samples were 10 to 100 times higher than concentrations detected in breast milk from women living in Europe. Studies show that most Americans may already carry levels of PBDEs that have been found to cause serious, permanent neurological damage in laboratory animals. A particular hot spot for PBDEs in fish is San Francisco Bay. PCBs, it seems, are being replaced by an equally toxic and nearly identical compound.

In late June 2010, I flew to Greenland to attend the Inuit Circumpolar Council (ICC). Greenland would seem a strange place to end a story that began in the warm, turquoise waters of the Bahamas. Sadly, it's a logical extension. The oceans are constantly moving and mixing, and contaminants are distributed worldwide on the currents and winds. The trip was prompted by the fact that Inuit peoples who inhabit the arctic region from Alaska, across Canada, Greenland, and northern Russia exhibit the highest levels of POP contamination on earth. Winds distribute chemical effluent generated in industrial nations preferentially into the northern regions. The toxins' effect is magnified because the aboriginal peoples of the North eat large quantities of marine mammals, which eat prey that has biomagnified contaminants in the food web. These people are thus superapex predators, ingesting the highest concentrations of these chemicals.

As my IcelandAir flight slipped out of U.S. airspace, bound for Greenland, I was anxiously waiting for word on the International Whaling Commission's response to Greenland's request to kill humpback whales for aboriginal subsistence.

Once we were over water beyond Labrador, the ocean remained cloud covered the entire way to Iceland. An hour out of Keflavík, I realized the humpbacks that could well become targets of Greenlander harpoons were swimming a vertical mile away. I've known this stock of whales in the Caribbean at Samaná Bay and out on the Silver Bank. They were extraordinarily friendly toward me in the water when I was filming. Along most of their migratory route off the eastern seaboard of the United States, the humpbacks are protected. Since gaining this protection, they've become increasingly friendly and curious toward the whale watchers who now constitute a multimillion-dollar business for charter boat owners, hotels, and restaurants.

The knowledge that twenty-seven of these curious, intelligent, infinitely graceful, and now trusting creatures will be killed after years of protection is appalling. I recalled a day when, while filming humpbacks off Moorea in French Polynesia, a female swam right up to me. She adjusted her massive body and lifted her flipper carefully over my head as she swam by no more than two meters away. She was conscious of my fragility and didn't want to harm me. The trust that has developed between human and whale in many parts of the world now seems destined to be breached.

Aboriginal hunts of marine mammals are a highly complex ethical issue. There is no denying the Inuit and their cousins have traditionally thrived on what they call "natural food" – caribou, seal, beluga, whales, and other marine mammals. But times have changed. While in Greenland I would find out just how much.

During my stopover in Iceland, I learned that the IWC had indeed voted to allow Greenland a quota of twenty-seven humpback whales to be taken by aboriginal people and used solely for aboriginal purposes. This body of men and women in suits, including the U.S. delegation, sitting in a windowless hall voted to allow the slaughter of the great white-winged singers of the seas.

This was not my first visit to the land of the Inuit. I spent some time among them in Iqaluit in Nunavut, a federal territory in Canada with quite a measure of independence from Ottawa. I learned that when aboriginal peoples change their diet from "natural" foods to store-bought processed foods and fast foods, they develop diseases ranging from acne to diabetes and obesity. And buying food costs money. Hunting costs much less. But hunting beluga, narwhal, pilot whales, and other cetaceans is no longer a viable means of putting food on the table. Contaminant levels are simply too high.

While in Nuuk, Greenland, I discovered the whalers are not observing the terms of the IWC quota that allows the aboriginal hunt. Greenlanders already hunt fin and minke whales under IWC quota but the hunt is as much about profits as it is about aboriginal rights. Whales taken by Greenlanders are less and less destined for an aboriginal table. I got a tip from Sue Fisher of the Whale and Dolphin Conservation Society that one of its agents had discovered whale meat being sold in high-end restaurants and markets in Ilulissat at very high prices. I decided to check out Nuuk to see if I could find similar out-of-quota sales. It wasn't difficult and doesn't qualify me as a double-O agent. I took my iPhone, put it on video, and entered the main supermarket. Right there in the meat section, just by the sausages, were piles of two-pound packages of whale meat. I asked the desk clerk at my hotel if I might find whale meat in a restaurant. She cheerily told me the Thai restaurant next door had whale sushi and named a couple of other possibilities. Sure enough, the Thai restaurant had the whale sushi and something called Mekong River Whale Whiskey soup. Later, I documented whale steak in a greasy-spoon burger/pizza joint.

When I broke this story on Twitter, I had no idea the word would resound in Nuuk so quickly. A local radio reporter chased me down and interviewed me about my "undercover" videotaping of the whale meat. He'd done a brief story on my activities and apparently, I was the talk of the town. He put the interview on the air and on the radio station's much read Internet site. The next day, I felt a distinct chilling in the way the Inuit responded to me.

On the last day of the ICC, a young Inuit from eastern Greenland told me pleadingly that his village needed to take whales outside the IWC quota. "We steal them," he admitted, meaning they were taking whales in a manner that was not permitted.

"What species of whale are you taking?" I asked.

"Any kind that the elders tell us," was his reply.

In reality, the Inuit of Greenland may be having a hard time getting any whale meat because the big-money guys are sucking it all up for the more lucrative commercial trade.

Humpbacks had been missing from Greenlandic waters for sixty years—hunted out by European whalers. Their population has now recovered to the extent that explorer whales have made their way back to ancient feeding grounds. This should be cause for joyous celebration, not a dreadful slaughter.

One of my main purposes in going to Greenland was to look into one of the more startling results of contamination of the marine environment. Among the most perverse effects of estrogen-imitating chemicals such as PCBs and dioxins is that they seem to have increased the ratio of girl babies to boy babies born to Inuit mothers who consume marine mammal meat. But exactly what is going on is open to interpretation. At first glance, there is an increase in the number of girls born. But something even stranger may be taking place. My oncologist at the Mayo Clinic in Jacksonville tells me the high levels of estrogen-like chemicals do not actually change the sex of boys to that of girls. They do not turn XY into XX. What is happening is that the phony estrogen may only be changing the sexual organs and secondary sexual characteristics of boys into those of girls. So the Inuit and other arctic peoples may have boys who appear to be girls. This obviously demands further study, but the need to stop eating food that can radically skew the sex ratios of a population is not something to debate. Despite the abundant information available, I found the Inuit in complete denial that there was any problem whatsoever with eating marine mammal meat. They consider the meat of beluga and narwhals and whales to be "natural." Thus, *ipso facto*, it cannot be anything but good. They just don't want to think about the chemicals.

When I asked the same young man who had told me of "stealing whales" about the gender bending chemicals that had altered the sex ratio of births in Inuit villages, he told me he was aware of this. He then dismissed these ominous facts by saying, "It happens in Inuit villages in Russia too." For him the fact that the phenomenon was widespread seemed to make it all okay.

On the flight home I couldn't help but wonder, "What will it take to get *homo sapiens*, (self-named Man the Wise), to stop poisoning ourselves and all the other living creatures of our planet?" In my opinion, the answer is catastrophe, events so horrifying that they prod people from their personal and familiar concerns to involvement in the wider world on which we all depend for survival, then demand change from politicians and business. We have no lack of such catastrophes. Minamata is one example and the massive oil spill in the Gulf of Mexico another. Those are only two and surely more are on the way. But this is not a hopeless situation, although it grows more serious by the day. The European Union has led the way in reducing the production, use and disposal of toxic chemicals. Legislation is being introduced in the United States and, ironically, may be advanced by the ghastly results of the Gulf oil spill.

Although catastrophes seem to assault us from all points of the compass, we do not need to seek solutions for each problem. We need to change our attitudes from seeking to maximize profits at any cost to making the health of humanity, other animals with whom we share the earth and waters, and the entire life support system of this planet an absolute first priority. If that system collapses, there will be no profits for anyone.

As we conduct our daily work when back at the BlueVoice office in St. Augustine, we receive information via Twitter, Facebook, e-mail, YouTube, and many other sources, virtually all of them electronic and delivered in ways unimagined only a decade ago. The information arrives on my desktop computer, iPhone, and iPad. Reports come from Taiji and elsewhere in Japan, from Greenland, the coast of Ireland, from the Gulf of Mexico and from the Faroe Islands. And they come from just up the road along our northeast Florida coast where fish kills, algal blooms, and an unusual number of dolphin deaths tell us of the immediacy of the crisis we face in the oceans.

We constantly transmit information, video or photographs of events such as the slaughter of dolphins in Japan, the illegal whale meat in Nuuk, and data on contamination levels. We can have it on the Internet within moments from remote parts of the earth. We reach thousands of interested people with urgent information they can act on in nearly real time.

The forces of destruction of the ocean and its creatures are massive and well funded. But the new technologies give us a tool that can bring awareness and organizational power to millions of people on a global scale. Feedback from tens of thousands through the networking sites tells me of the growing concern and passion for the oceans and its creatures, especially the whales and dolphins. It is our challenge to elevate that awareness to effective action.

During my years of studying dolphins in the open sea, I have seen myriad examples of their intelligence and willingness to communicate. Over time, we will expand our communication with these marvelous creatures in ways yet unknown. But until the day comes when the dolphins can speak for themselves, we must be their voices.

Epilogue

I write the final words of this book while at anchor a couple miles off Bimini. Late yesterday we headed out of Miami through Government Cut on the 104-foot schooner *Juliet.* A pod of bottlenose dolphins was feeding about ten miles offshore. They came to our bow and rode with us for nearly an hour. Crossing the Gulf Stream can bring surprises at any moment—pods of pilot whales, sperm whales, and pelagic dolphins. The Gulf Stream is, for me, a dividing line between the world of petty pace and a magical blue-green universe peopled by curious and friendly aliens who are not merely the product of fertile imaginations.

But in this summer of 2010, we are alert for evidence that oil from the Deepwater Horizon disaster has entered the Gulf Stream to threaten even the remote areas of the Bahamas where we encounter the dolphins. So far we have found no traces of it.

This is the thirty-second summer since we first found the *Maravilla* dolphins in 1978. Since then, we have found other friendly dolphins. Each pod has individual responses to our presence in the water. Dolphins on White Sand Ridge, where we made first contact, are today so habituated to human presence that they spend a lot of their time interacting with us and other parties that venture out there. The same is true of the spotted dolphins off Bimini who are frequently visited. On many occasions, they approach us so closely that it's impossible to film them. But that's fine. Being with them without the obligation to film is a blessing.

At another location—I won't disclose its coordinates—spotted dolphins are less accustomed to interacting with people but still eager to introduce themselves and tolerant of our presence so we're able to photograph true natural history behavior. And I have learned of yet another pod of spotters totally naïve of humans and yet quite accessible. So we set out looking for new friends and to demonstrate that the dolphins of White Sand Ridge, rather than being unique, are representative of pretty much all dolphins around the world: friendly, curious, and social when approached in a respectful manner.

During our previous two voyages, we have seen new and astonishing behavior from the spotted dolphins. After more than thirty years, these brilliant animals still manage to delight and inspire. Late one afternoon, we came upon them feeding on juvenile yellowtail. The dolphins tore into the fish ball, snapping up one yellowtail after another. The fish were terrified. That was clear in their eyes and I felt compassion for them. The fish saw our bodies as sanctuaries and were especially drawn to the cleavage exposed by the women swimmers' bathing suits. They would dive in seeking safety, but the dolphins were in no way constrained by this tactic, nor any sense of propriety, and gently plucked the fish from the women's suits. Dolphin lovers though they are, the women were out of the water quickly.

"I want to be close to the dolphins but enough is enough," said one well-endowed woman as she pulled off her mask and snorkel.

As always, I hope to find Chopper. He had not been seen after massive hurricanes, far more powerful than the one we'd survived in 1983, ripped through White Sand Ridge in 2004 and 2005. Many of the spotted dolphins identified over decades have not been seen again and are thought to have perished. But in 2008, Denise Herzing, a dedicated researcher who spends countless weeks with the spotters each summer, told me she had seen him. Chopper still lives—now thirty-one years old.

Author on diver propulsion vehicle "flies" with the dolphins
© Hardy Jones Productions, 1989 Photo from video by Marty Snyderman

I observed the seventh anniversary of my diagnosis of multiple myeloma in late spring of 2010. While I have not been cured of the disease, my blood and urine indicators remain at essentially the same levels as after my first month on thalidomide and dexamethasone. I've switched to a new drug—Revlimid, which is an advanced version of thalidomide. My dosages are very low but the dexamethasone still gives me speedy high energy followed by precipitous drops. I have to plan life around these fluctuations.

There are many plan B myeloma treatment regimens, different "cocktails" of drugs that I've never had to try. Some are proving extremely effective. There's an advanced version of Revlimid in the pipeline. One combination of drugs is now producing a few molecular remissions—remissions so strong that the myeloma cannot be found by the most sophisticated tests. But these are strong drugs, and as long as I remain stable,

I will probably not resort to them. More and more, multiple myeloma is considered a chronic disease for many patients rather than a death sentence.

My hope remains to both save dolphins from spears and toxic chemicals and to help awaken people to the deadly threat of contaminants we pour daily into the world's rivers, lakes and oceans. In that manner I hope to do my small part to help prevent cancer—a far better path than spending hundreds of millions of dollars finding a cure for it.

While I don't feel the energy I did at age thirty, or even age fifty, I still work a full schedule, walk my dog, do some body surfing, occasional yoga and travel with Deborah to international meetings and film shoots.

I continue to work on the film we've titled *Our Shared Fate.* Its premise has changed. At first, I thought of finding connections between marine contamination, disease in dolphins, and areas of high incidence of multiple myeloma. But as I penetrated deeper into the issue, I found the problem of ocean contamination by heavy metals and organic pollutants to be far more sinister and ubiquitous than I'd imagined when I began. It is clear that these chemicals assail the most fundamental mechanisms of life.

Being with dolphins, sperm whales, and orcas in the majesty of the open sea, feeling myself the object of their curiosity and their mental processing, knowing there are life forms on earth extraordinarily similar, yet not identical to me, is inspirational. These experiences expand my sense of what the universe is and who populates it.

Version two of our white paper is in production. Alarmingly, it will be vastly larger than the one we published only three years ago. It will be ready to present at the next meeting of the IWC in July 2011. Our films *The Dolphin Defender* and *When Dolphins Cry* still run on international broadcasts, and we love getting e-mails from passionately dedicated viewers from all over the globe.

We continue to work to end the killing of dolphins in Japan. I now know that simply exposing its barbarity will not end it. But other tactics exist, ones I can't reveal now but will update on BlueVoice.org as they move from the planning to the execution stage. In Japan there is exciting news. Japanese environmental groups are forming and growing, not just to protect dolphins and whales but the ocean itself. BlueVoice is supporting these NGOs with historical information on whaling and dolphin hunting as well as information on toxins in the marine food chain. Sakae has started a website for Japanese children and we support her efforts fully. And perhaps our continuing efforts to inform the Japanese people of the dangers of mercury are paying off. Demand for whale meat is falling precipitously and the number of dolphins killed in 2010 – 2011 is far below average. On many days the dolphin hunters did not venture out. Still, hundreds of dolphins die an agonizing death in the killing cove at Taiji.

BlueVoice is now preparing an expedition to the Silver Bank north of the Dominican Republic where the humpbacks of the northeast Atlantic congregate during the winter to mate and give birth before returning to the coasts of New England, Newfoundland and Greenland. Our purpose is to make a film to present at the 2011 IWC to argue against the quota that allows Greenland to hunt these animals.

Despite the challenges, I imagine a world in which we apply the ethics of the ancient Greeks, who considered killing a dolphin to be an act of murder. We must not only not kill dolphins and whales and other large-brained animals, we must respect them and the life support system that sustains their lives. The only way we can do that is to safeguard vast areas of habitat on the land and in the oceans. Of course, if we do this we will safeguard our own health and that of our children.

Beyond that, we can have relationships with intelligent, curious, and friendly creatures who can enrich our experience of what it is to be human.

So this book is finished but I hope those of you as passionately interested in dolphins, whales and the oceans as I am will see this work as a portal to the continued unfolding of the stories told here. Updates will appear on bluevoice.org and on a blog I'll establish to deal solely with the material in this book.

Outside my cabin a nearly full moon hangs at sixty degrees off the horizon. I climb into my bunk with the prayer, "Tomorrow, let there be dolphins."

11575134R0015